MY MOTHER'S EYES

HOLOCAUST MEMORIES OF A YOUNG GIRL

By Anna Ornstein

Illustrations by Stewart Goldman

books

My Mother's Eyes
Copyright Anna Ornstein, Stewart Goldman 2004

Published by Emmis Books
1700 Madison Road
Cincinnati, OH 45206

ISBN 157860-145-2

Library of Congress number TK

Cover design: Dana Boll
Interior design: Dana Boll

1 2 3 4 5 6 7 8 9 10

Anna's Dedication

This book is dedicated to my husband,
my children, grandchildren, and to the memory
of my family and all those who did not return.

Stewart's Dedication

In memory of my grandmother Anna Porter
whose roots in the Ukraine led me to explore
the Holocaust in my image making.

Table of Contents

sky

—

PREFACE

The stories presented here depict how a seventeen-year-old Jewish girl from Hungary experienced her childhood against the backdrop of Hungarian anti-Semitism and a long and bitter war. The immediacy and unembellished simplicity of her narratives draw her readers into these experiences as if they had been there. We are with her at every turn as she recreates the escalating terror from the time of the German occupation of Hungary, to the swift incarceration of the Jews in ghettos, to the vicissitudes of her various camp experiences, to the unexpected day of liberation, and finally to our miraculous reunion. It is with the eyes of a seventeen year old but with the style and maturity that comes with age and with the distance from those events that she makes us part of her experiences.

Although Anna Ornstein's physical survival was a quirk of fate, her emotional survival with the fullness of her love of life, of her dreams and ambitions intact, was not. These tales, and the way she wrote them, reflect this. In August of 1945, when Anna and her mother returned from concentration camp, she told me in great detail, over a period of several weeks, about her camp experiences, and I told her about mine in a forced labor battalion. Soon, the joint rebuilding of our lives and planning for the future took center stage. Anna focused on completing her interrupted schooling, on becoming a physician, then a psychiatrist, child psychiatrist and psychoanalyst, while mothering our three children.

Anna frequently spoke to our children about her family.

She told them about her pre-Shoah experiences growing up in a small village in Hungary, and whenever the children would ask, she would offer snippets of her camp experiences. She also felt free to talk about these events to friends, if they asked. It was never a main topic of conversation.

The writing of these tales is a story in itself. Passover had been one of our favorite holidays, especially since the time when our children could enjoy their participation in it. When our daughter Sharone came home for Seder as a freshman in college, she wanted to create a new way for everyone around the table to participate. She asked each of us to say something about what freedom meant to us personally. This is when Anna wrote her first Passover story. She read it at the table after the children found the *afikoman* and the calm and serenity of the Seder were restored. Everyone responded with stunned silence—teary-eyed and appreciative that Anna shared with us a small, circumscribed slice of her camp experiences.

This became a yearly event for the next twenty-five years. At every Seder there was a new story—a new, hitherto untold moment from the past. The anticipatory curiosity has never waned. Anna, experiencing the response of her children, other members of the family, and untold number of our friends, was motivated to write them by her desire to leave a legacy about our destroyed families to our children and grandchildren. These stories, then, became a part of our Haggada, which tells of persecution, slavery and redemption—they were to help the young maintain their own sense of continuity, on which our Jewish survival depends.

She would begin to write one of these tales shortly before every Passover. Each story captured a specific moment; each appeared to have emerged afresh, as if it had been recalled for the first time. The various episodes were originally composed at random but when they were arranged for publication, they were placed in chronological sequence. In this form, in their aggregate, the stories offer a coherent, representative picture of Anna's pre-Shoah experiences, along with those in the camps and some that followed later. Though highly personal, they also portray the fate of other surviving Hungarian Jewish teenagers of her generation. For this reason, a quick glance at the history of the Jews of Hungary should broaden the context for Anna's personal experiences, since these stories are now presented here for a larger audience.

* * *

Jews had already lived in communities, organized around their synagogues, prior to the arrival of the Magyars, in the territory of what later became Hungary. The oldest tombstone from the third century attests to the fact that the Romans found the Jews there when they conquered the region. The persecution of the Jews began around the first millennium, as soon as King Stephen I converted the pagan Magyars to Christianity while the Jews refused conversion. They paid dearly for this refusal. From then on, for almost another millennium, about every three hundred years, the history of the Jews in Hungary was punctuated by pogroms, massacres, and expulsions with serious curtailment of their freedom and livelihood. They were often robbed of all their belongings, massacred, and those who survived were brutally expelled. Later they were invited back when needed to lift the economic conditions of an impoverished country. Each time they returned, they would do well for the country. Their successes, however, would evoke the wrath of the populace again, and another brutal expulsion would follow; the sequence would be repeated again and again, with longer or shorter intervals. A number of unusually fruitful periods of collaboration also occurred, during which the Jews were lulled into believing in the permanence of their newly won status. Conversion always opened some doors, at least temporarily. This cooperation encouraged large-scale assimilation by the Jews, in the hope of gaining acceptance as full-fledged citizens under the law.

This acceptance eventually happened in 1849, under Franz Joseph, who was the Monarch of the Austro-Hungarian Empire from 1848 to 1916. Though the Jews as a religious group did not receive equal rights until as late 1895, the brief period from 1849 to 1914 is justifiably regarded as the Golden Age of Hungarian Jewry. From the eighteenth and early nineteenth centuries on, even before they obtained equal rights, the Jews had made enormous contributions, well beyond their percentage of the population, toward bringing Hungary from a backward, agricultural society into the modern industrial age. They established financial institutions and large-scale industrial concerns, modernized agriculture, established domestic and international commerce, made noteworthy contributions to art, literature, science, medicine and the law. During the very short span of time between 1849 and 1914, their contributions to all those areas increased manifold. While assimilation increased, so did the Jews' attention to their own history and culture bringing forth unrivaled scholarship in their own institutions of higher learning as well as in the country's universities. It seemed as if finally, in spite of an ever-present anti-Semitism, not only a temporary accommodation but a fruitful symbiosis between the Jews and the non-Jews could be established. Large numbers of Jews fought in WW I on the side of the Austro-Hungarian Empire with enthusiasm and bravery.

This symbiosis, however, was short-lived. The empire lost the war, and the ensuing anarchy brought a bloody communist regime to power. Since many of the leaders of this transient communist regime were Jews, Admiral Horthy's counterrevolution—the white terror—also engulfed the Jews as scapegoats. Pogroms, oppressions and persecutions were rampant again. The Horthy regime exploited the ever-present anti-Semitism of the populace to its own political ends and in 1920 introduced the first discriminatory law against Jews in twentieth-century Europe: the "numerus clausus," which restricted entrance to universities and high schools. From 1920 on, through the next decade and a half, the life of Jews had slowly but progressively become more constrained. Although we lived in a country still governed by laws, in practice we no longer lived as equals under the law. In 1933, after Hitler's ascent to power in Germany, the Hungarian anti-Semites became more vocal and more powerful, and they began to demand further curtailments against the Jews. They became stronger in the National Parliament and demanded the elimination of the Jews from civil service, the army, and the professions. They wished to re-segregate them in ghettos and ultimately expel them.

The Hungarian Jews could not hear this as a wake-up call. Most of them considered these excesses as lunacy that ultimately would stop. Most of them could not imagine that Hungary could regress to an earlier mode of primitive, murderous rage against a valuable segment of its population with impeccable patriotic credentials. Most Hungarian Jews fought Zionism as a possible solution to their plight, while it might still have been possible to emigrate to Palestine.

Then, in 1938, the first anti-Jewish law was enacted in Parliament, designed to force the Jews from the economy. The second one, more severe, was enacted in 1939, designed to limit Jews in gaining ground in public life and in the economy. In this law the Jews were also declared unfit for the military, which later justified the establishment of paramilitary forced labor camps. As if these two laws had not done enough harm, a third one was enacted in 1940 to protect the purity of the Aryan race. It forbade marriages between Jews and non-Jews. In the next step, the Hungarians enthusiastically joined Hitler's project of the Final Solution.

At this point, assimilation in Hungary was bankrupt. But already in the late 1920's and certainly by the 1930's, disappointments in the results of assimilation gave some room for the spread of Zionism among Hungarian Jews. Anna and I were fortunate to grow up with the Zionist ideals. For our generation of young Jews, these were emotional antidotes, because we did not know a period in Hungary without discrimination, without episodic harassment, and severe economic hardships. So, for us, it was easy to renounce the Hungarian patriotism of earlier generations of Jews, to nurture a strong Zionist identification, and to look to the future outside of the borders of Nazi Hungary.

This outlook gave us inner strength to withstand daily humiliations, even physical pain and hunger. In labor camps, such resiliency of spirit could be life saving—it was a bulletproof vest against the atrocities perpetrated against us. It helped us remember who we were, the pride we could feel in being Jewish, in being a link in countless generations of the people of the book, that had survival value under these circumstances. This gift our families transmitted to us made it possible for Anna to survive with the fullness of her love of life, of her dreams and ambitions intact. Her stories, and the spirit they express, are testimonies to the importance of these values for the emotional survival of one Hungarian Jewish girl among many.

Paul Ornstein

INTRODUCTION

THE VOICE OF MEMORY

Year after year we sit around the Seder table and read the familiar stories of slavery and the exodus from Egypt. Year after year, we tell the story of the most recent slavery, recount our sorrows over the losses we suffered and speak of our deliverance.

During the last few years, each time Passover neared, I decided not to write another story. But each time I changed my mind. I believe I cannot stop writing because these stories are memorials I am erecting in the minds of our children. I fear that if I stop writing, stop building the memorial, my children and everyone who reads these stories, will stop remembering the people we have lost—and those who are forgotten are truly dead.

We are grandparents now. We have four very handsome grandsons and one beautiful granddaughter. When I look at them and delight in the sparks in their eyes and in their healthy minds and bodies, it is then that I am particularly grateful for the memories, the images I retained of my parents and my brothers. As I look at my grandchildren, the memories of the past are becoming stronger not dimmer.

James E. Young calls the insistence of memorializing the Holocaust the "missing gravestone syndrome." "In keeping with the bookish, iconoclastic side of Jewish tradition" he says, "the first memorials of the Holocaust period came not in stone, glass and steel but in narrative. The 'Yizkhor Bicher'—memorial books—remembered both, the lives and the destruction of

European Jewish communities according to the most ancient of Jewish memorial media: words on paper. For a murdered people without graves, without even corpses to inter, memorial books often came to serve as symbolic tombstones."[1]

Memories, shared memories in particular, have an immensely cathartic effect. Think of the reaction survivors had to *Schindler's List*. Many people were puzzled and could not understand why survivors were so pleased to see a movie that they found horrifying and which made them sick. Our friends thought it would be difficult for us to see images that would remind us of our experiences in the camps. What our friends may not have realized is that these images did not come to us unexpectedly; we live with these memories every day. Also, what is often not recognized is that there is triumph in surviving. For me, most important in watching the movie was that it made it possible to share memories that have otherwise been difficult to put into words. Movies, as other forms of art (literature, music, painting), are vehicles of communication; they are products of memory that had undergone transformation by the artist's vision. Artists and writers, because of their special skills and talents, are able to communicate feelings that those of us not blessed with special gifts are unable to articulate. This is why survivors said that in addition to the 12 Oscars for which *Schindler's List* was nominated, they would have liked to add a number of newly created categories: The Most Wrenching, The Most Cathartic and The Most Accessible Treatment of an Impossible Subject.

Our memories had become links that connect us to the past as well as to the future: the stories our children hear about their grandparents, their aunts and uncles anchor them in their own past. But memories can only be shared with those we expect will listen with respect and understanding. The image of the camp is so appalling that our listeners often suffer a small trauma once they permit the meaning of what they hear to penetrate. People rightfully, naturally and expectedly shut out from their awareness feelings that can, potentially, be disorganizing to them. Anything connected to the Holocaust—most importantly the cold-blooded murder of millions—brings with it horror too large and intensely personal to confront with equanimity. As we tell the story, resistance to hearing it will come up in many ways. This is how our daughter Miriam expressed her reaction to hearing the stories when she was 14 years old:

16

When people speak of
the Holocaust
I think of my parents
My mother was in Auschwitz twice
But I can't connect the
Two …

The mother I know
is not the same
person who experienced
those horrors ….
saw the gaschambers,
lived in a ghetto
not my mother …

Once our listeners are able to make the connection between us and the horrors they hear, they frequently say that we must be special. But there is nothing special about survivors; none of us is in the possession of special powers. Those who have not been tried have no way of knowing their own resources, their own capacities for survival.

We are a link in the chain of generations of Jewish people. It is in us and through us that much of this dreadful period of our past is alive. Making our experiences relevant to the next generation, we keep those alive whose passing we shall never stop to commemorate. Nothing can be more rewarding than to know that the memories we share with our children were received with love and compassion; to know that the link we forged between our two generations will be enduring. I am quoting Miriam again who wrote this little poem after a discussion about the Holocaust in Religious School.

I am so angry
I felt like screaming,
You are taking part of
me, of my life
and trying to put into words
and theories

When my father went
back to his hometown
the temple was gone,
a warehouse was in its place
my father never cries
but when he saw his temple
destroyed
a part of him died ....

Now and then an image
comes to my mind
of a temple
burned out, missing a wall
the broken shape of a
Jewish star
mutilated.

I know little about the lives of my grandparents but the
vague knowledge I had about their perseverance and their
determination to create as good a life for their families as was
possible in the hostile environments in which they lived, that
knowledge, was a source of inspiration to me. I always knew
about their love of learning, whether this concerned Jewish
learning or studies in medical school, or just to read and write
for the pleasure of it. The way these people lived their lives
was an inspiration, a "beacon in the sky" for me. They had
powerfully influenced the person I had become.

Our lives are finite, but books, letters, pictures and stories
told by parents to their children go on living. But more than
the written word, traditions that carry attitudes and values
become built into the deepest layers of our personalities. For our
grandchildren, the glow of the Friday night candles, the blessing
over vine and chalah[2], the yearly Seder nights with family and
friends may become associated with a feeling of belonging not
only to a caring and loving family but also to a larger cultural and
ethnic community. For us, personally, these experiences and this
sense of belonging had great survival value.

[1] *The Texture of Memory* James E. Young, Yale U. Press, 1993.

[2] A special braided bread for Shabbat.

MY FAVORITE MEMORIES

The streets were unpaved. There were no sidewalks. In the fall and winter, there was mud and snow on the ground; in the summer, there was dust everywhere. We drew water from an uncovered well in the middle of the marketplace. As in other small towns in rural Hungary, there was neither electricity nor a water system.

I was born and grew up in the small agricultural village called Szendro in northern Hungary. About four thousand people lived there, mainly peasants. Among them—though socially and culturally a world apart—lived forty Jewish families: shopkeepers, a tailor, a roofer, a shoemaker, a doctor, and a pharmacist. The village did not have a high school, a library, or a hospital. The city with these "luxuries" was forty kilometers away, over an hour by train. We only went to the city on special occasions or in the case of a medical emergency.

There were three one-room elementary schools in Szendro: a Catholic, a Jewish, and a Protestant, each next to its place of worship. From an early age, the people of the village were segregated according to their religion.

Our house, a large L-shaped, two-family home, dominated the center of the village. The house was built on the grounds of a burned-out castle. The castle, a heavy stone structure, remained standing without its roof and served as a playground for the children in the village.

The yard, with its garden and stacks of lumber, was closed off from the rest of the village by a large iron gate and was

protected by a guard dog. Once inside the house, one forgot
that this was a home in a small village. Each room had a tall
tile stove, and the dining room had handsome furniture and
an Oriental rug. Most importantly, the shelves were stacked
with books by French, Hungarian, Russian, and German
authors. My father was particularly proud of his collection of
German books. He received a German newspaper weekly so as
not to forget the fine German he spoke. I still regret that we,
his children, refused to learn by heart his favorite poems by
Goethe and Schiller.

But the minds and the temperaments of the children of
the village were not only shaped by their experiences inside
their homes. Powerful influences were exerted on us by the
people amongst whom we lived. That influence came mainly
from the Gypsies, who built their mud houses outside of the
village. In the spring and fall and when it was not too hot in
the summer, the Gypsies camped out on the steps in front
of our house: the women nursing their babies, the children
playing, the men tuning and playing their violins. The only
entertainment the children had in the village was provided
by the Gypsies. We looked forward to the occasions when
they would make music, such as during the peasant weddings,
where the music usually lasted through the night. We never
went into the homes or yards where the weddings took place,
because people could become boisterous, even dangerous, on
such occasions. The Hungarian peasants liked their red wine.
But the music spilled out into the street, and that was where we
had our own party. We danced for hours and rarely went home
of our own free will. Either our older siblings or our parents
would come and fetch us. Hot and exhausted, we begged to

stay. We hated to go home before the music had died down
completely.

By the time I was eleven years old, in 1941, Jews could not
have household help. It was then, as the only girl in my family,
that I was introduced to doing household chores. I helped my
mother bake bread, wash dishes, scrub floors, do laundry. I
remember how proud I was when I was able to carry not one
but two pails of water from the well. On Friday afternoons, I
looked forward to the house smelling clean, the laundry being
done, the beds freshly made. I was particularly eager to scrub
the floor in the kitchen, the sun room and the porch in the back
of the house, because my father found special delight in seeing
the shine come back in the colorful patterns of the stone tiles,
as if they had just been freshly laid. My cheeks burned from
being hot and tired, but I was very pleased with myself.

In 1941 my two brothers, Paul and Andrew, lived in the
city, each attending a different high school, one a Catholic, the
other a Protestant gymnasium. The "numerus clauses," the law
forbidding Jews to attend non-Jewish schools, was in effect by
then and was applied to high schools as well as universities,
but a few Jewish students were admitted if they passed a rather
rigorous entrance examination. Whenever the boys were due
to come home, Mother took out a white tablecloth, and the
house would be filled with the smell of chicken soup. I loved
to change into my Shabbat clothes and put on my white knee
socks, which looked good with my navy-blue pleated skirt and
white cotton blouse. The freshly scrubbed look was complete
with my hair pulled back tightly and fixed into two shoulder-
length braids. When the boys came home, they too changed
into their Shabbat clothes and we would go to Grandmother's

so she could bless us before the men of the house went to temple.

For me, this was the high point of the day. Grandmother was a tiny woman; we had to bend down so she could put her hands over our heads. I still can see her crooked fingers and hear her murmur the blessings: "Be like Rebecca, Rachel and Leah...." She kissed our foreheads, and we were free to leave. Though this was a ritual, it was never done routinely but always with great seriousness and dignity. When the boys were home, my mother's mood changed drastically; her sons were her best company. My mother and my brother Paul were particularly close friends. Both were bright, quick-tempered, and held strong opinions. They argued heatedly over nearly any subject. Their conversations were always exciting and the outcome rarely predictable. I see them going for walks, with arms linked, hotly debating Marx, Lenin, and the impact of the French Revolution on the rest of Europe. I frequently went along on these walks, but I never became part of the conversation. I was in awe of all the things they seemed to know.

I have many memories of times we spent in the kitchen. The pots on the wood-burning stove gave off enough steam to make the kitchen reasonably warm in the wintertime. Andrew, my younger brother, who was seventeen in 1941, would bring out his favorite poetry book, the poems by Jozsef Atilla, the discontented revolutionary poet who was our hero in those days. Andrew would read the poems aloud, mother interrupting him from time to time to correct his diction or to emphasize a special point. We knew most of the poems by heart.

When the boys left home, life moved slowly again. We

made every effort to make our days normal and tried to avoid becoming too deeply affected by the news that more and more of my brothers' contemporaries were being called into forced labor camps. We had very little access to news from the front, but what we read in our papers was very discouraging. The news of the German troops rapidly advancing on the eastern front deepened our fears and sense of insecurity. We knew we were trapped. The days when the family was together and we succeeded in creating a sense of safety inside our home were like small islands in a turbulent sea on which we took brief, transitory rests.

oven

—

DANCING THE HORA

I always loved to dance, a legacy of the Gypsy music I heard so often in my life. Shabbat afternoons, when there was absolutely nothing to do in our small God-forsaken village, we went on long walks or gathered in each other's homes and spent hours dancing. Without the benefit of Gypsy music, we sang the popular songs of the day and learned to dance the tango, the fox-trot and the waltz. But more often than not, we danced the hora. We created endless variations on this traditional folk dance that filled us with excitement and what we believed to be the Zionist spirit.

Our hopes for the future seemed to have run on two parallel but not readily reconcilable tracks: on the one hand, we dreamed about building a Jewish state in Palestine; on the other hand, we studied Latin and algebra as if the doors of the universities suddenly would open to Jewish boys and girls.

I don't believe my parents were particularly ambitious for me to get an advanced education. Nevertheless, when I left Szendro in 1942 at the age of fifteen to live with my aunt in Debrecen to help her with her new-born baby, they did not object to my efforts to get into the Jewish gymnasium there. This all-boy school had opened its doors to girls because fewer and fewer Jewish girls were admitted to non-Jewish college preparatory schools. I very much wanted to be taught by "real" teachers. My mother taught me during my first four years of high school education, which was not college-preparatory, offering only basic math and none of the classics. Every June, at the end of the school year, I took an examination in the school of the nearest city and received credit for the academic year. Should I be admitted to the gymnasium, I would be taught by real teachers, and I would have regular school hours. After a year of study, I passed the entrance examination and was admitted to the Jewish gymnasium in Debrecen.

I was poorly prepared for the rigors of a school where students had been studying Latin, French, and algebra for the previous four years, but to be a student in this prestigious school was a great privilege, and I set out to prove that I deserved it. However, my joy in attending a school with teachers and classmates was short-lived. Less than two years later, the German army occupied Hungary.

It was late on a Sunday afternoon, March 19, 1944. The rather handsome building of the Jewish gymnasium was nearly empty, but dim light and quite a bit of noise came from one of the rooms on the second floor where our Zionist youth group held its weekly meetings. On this day, as on all such occasions, we discussed what we knew about life in Palestine, how the pioneers irrigated the swamps, how people lived on a kibbutz. After this serious part of the meeting, we sang Hebrew songs with fervor and conviction. At the end of the meeting, with total abandonment, we danced an exuberant and vigorous hora. We were in the middle of one of these lively, noisy horas when the door opened and a pale-faced man walked in. We stood still instantly. From the look on his face, we sensed that the man had bad news for us. He asked that we gather around him. In a low, hoarse voice he told us that the Germans had marched into Budapest that day and orders had been issued for Jews to remain wherever they happened to be. Roadblocks were already set up across the country, and Jews were forbidden to use public transportation. We dispersed immediately. I found my aunt nervously talking to the neighbors. The end was soon to come, but in what form, in what way, nobody knew.

The next day the Germans occupied Debrecen. Pretending that life could continue as before, I went to the home of my second-grade pupil, whom I tutored in reading and spelling. I recall walking home on that Monday night, the streets filled with German soldiers, whose faces I still remember. These soldiers were children, maybe sixteen or seventeen years old, and they were noisy and rowdy. Three or four of them would link arms and shove people off the sidewalk. My heart pounded in my throat, and I tried to melt into the wall as I made my way home in the dusk.

As I entered the house, my aunt took me to the bedroom and ordered me to get under the bed. Rumor had it that the Germans were picking up Jewish girls to take them to the front to be used as prostitutes by the German soldiers. We heard about these practices from my cousin, who had escaped from Czechoslovakia and at that time lived with us on false Arian papers. Lying under the bed I could barely breathe from fear.

As the noise subsided in the street, my aunt whisked me to the janitor's apartment. We hoped that I would be safe there, at least for this first night of the dreaded occupation.

pail

—

THE FAREWELL

The date was Monday, March 20, 1944. I remember the day and date so well because it was the day after the German army occupied Budapest. We went back to school but were tentative about it. Though our lives were totally disrupted, we were still trying, in a half-hearted way, to pretend that life could go on as before.

Students and professors acted equally anxious. Who could worry about Hungarian literature, history, or French? Rumors about atrocities in Budapest and the possibility of imminent deportation flew about wildly. Amid this atmosphere a man entered the classroom and called my name. He took me to the office to answer a phone call. I thought my parents must be calling. I expected them to call and tell me what I should do. Should I try to go home? Jews were not allowed to use public transportation, and I might be taken off the train. Should I risk that? Or should I stay in Debrecen and be separated from them at a time like this? But the phone call was not from my parents. I was seventeen years old in 1944, and my parents either expected me to know what I should do or they were too helpless themselves to help me make this decision.

The phone call was from my twenty-two-year-old brother, Paul. Where was he? Where was he calling from? How did he get to a phone? He had left home a few months earlier. Like all Jewish boys his age, he was in a forced labor camp, attached to a unit of the Hungarian army, doing their dirty work, like digging ditches and carrying heavy equipment. All I knew was that the call came from the train station in Debrecen, and since his transport had stopped there for a few hours, he managed to get to a phone.

"Can you come right away?" he asked.

I ran. I felt excited and, at the same time, apprehensive. Would I get to see him, or would I get there too late? Would they let me see him? Would I be picked up on my way? I don't remember if I took a bus or ran all the way. All I know is that I was filled with excitement at the thought of seeing him again and terribly afraid that I might not make it.

The next thing I remember is very vivid in my mind. I stood in the doorway of the station and looked out to the yard where trains idled, one beside the other. A uniformed man stood at the door. He was not a policeman or a soldier. He must have been a ticket seller or some other official of the station. In those days, we feared everybody in uniform. They all were our enemies. They asked for our papers at every turn, and we never could be sure what they might find wrong with them. The man at the door told me to go away, that I wasn't permitted to stay there. I knew that, I said, but did not move. The station seemed deserted. I don't remember anybody around. The man kept telling me to leave, but I was determined to stay and kept looking out to where the trains were standing.

And then I saw him—a figure crawling under the trains, wearing a heavy beige coat and a wool hat, carrying a pail in his hand. It was too warm for all that clothing, but one didn't leave belongings behind. He must be heading, I thought, toward the Russian front. I now could see that the figure definitely was my brother Paul. I felt terribly afraid that one of the trains might start moving with him under it. He must have been carrying the pail back and forth, pretending to carry water, hoping he would get to see me that way. The man at the door saw me watching the young man crawling under the trains. He kept telling me that I had to leave, but he didn't grab me and he didn't push me away.

Once Paul had managed to crawl beneath all the trains, he straightened up and moved quickly toward the station. I did not move because by then I realized that the man at the door knew what was happening, and if others at the station should see me he would have to chase me away. I waited till my brother stepped inside the station. We hugged each other tightly for a moment. I don't remember if we said anything to each other, maybe just something about him pretending to carry water so that he could see me. I remember tears in his eyes, but he also was smiling at me. He always smiled. Maybe that's why I don't remember him with just tears in his eyes.

Our meeting ended in a moment. We both were afraid the guards would find and punish him. He turned around and left. I don't remember him looking back at me. What I see in front of me now is the back of that light beige wool coat, and what is etched on my mind are the words I thought then: "This is the last time I shall see you." I hung around for a while, watching him crawl back to his train. Then he disappeared from sight. I thanked the man at the door for allowing me to stay in the station and explained that Paul was my brother, whom I loved very much.

My brother Paul did not return from the eastern front. To this day, I do not know how or where he died.

A VISIT

My memories following the occupation of Hungary remain particularly vivid in my mind. I remember that during those first days I wanted more than anything to go home. I wanted to be with my parents. In the direction of Szendro, however, there was a particularly dangerous roadblock on the bridge over the Tisza river. Some very clever plans had to be made to make this trip possible.

As the small towns were still free of German soldiers, and the tension in Debrecen grew heavier every day, my aunt decided that I ought to go to Hajdunanas, a small town near Debrecen where Paul's family, the family of my future husband, had lived. Paul was studying in Budapest at that time, but his two younger brothers, fourteen-year-old Zoli and twelve-year-old Tibi, were attending the Jewish gymnasium in Debrecen.

Friday afternoon, four days after Debrecen was occupied, Tibi came and proudly announced that he was charged with the task of taking me "home." This bright-eyed, intelligent little boy was five years my junior, but with his manner and quiet confidence he left no doubt as to who was in charge on this trip.

Though the train was already crowded when we arrived at the station, Tibi was determined to find a seat for me—and he did. As I squeezed into a tight spot, he remained standing next to me, protecting me from the crowd. Tibi was a dark-haired little fellow, full of energy and mischief. I looked up into his serious little face: shiny black hair, alert dark eyes. I was soon to learn that these features were definitely his mother's gifts to him.

We arrived in Hajdunanas after sunset. Paul's father was already in temple with Paul's youngest brother, five-year-old Lacika. Paul's mother, with table set and candles lit, was waiting for us. This was the first and only time I met Paul's mother: a beautiful but tired, worn-out woman. She suggested I eat some soup and go to bed right away. I still see the soup in front of me: a golden yellow chicken soup with eggs shirred into it—a fantastic treat in 1944! She must have gone to considerable trouble to find the eggs and to prepare such a meal for me. Her immediate comfort with me and mine with her, along with the Shabbat atmosphere in the home, relaxed the immense tension in my body, and I quickly fell asleep. Saturday is hazy in my mind, but I remember Sunday morning when I woke up and watched Paul's mother carrying a bundle of wood to make a fire. As I watched her kneel in front of the stove, I felt deep love and compassion for her. I was very pleased, when later in the day she asked me to darn some socks for Paul, as she was preparing to send a package to him and his sister Judit who also lived in Budapest.

As rumors spread that the Germans were expected in Hajdunanas the next day, I tried to get back to Debrecen in order to find a way to go home. Like two thieves, Paul's father—our children's dear Saba, the Grandpa—took me to the train station through some cornfields so that we would not be seen. Holding his hand, I felt his apprehension, and by now, I felt very much part of this family.

This was a visit never to be repeated, one that remains deeply etched in my mind as one of my precious and cherished

memories. Paul's father survived Mauthausen and returned
barely alive to Hungary in the summer of 1945. He made
aliyah in 1948 soon after the establishment of the State of
Israel, where he died in 1976. During these thirty years, he
never asked that we join him there. He respected his son's
decision to live in the United States. Nor did he waver in his
determination to take part in the building of a Jewish state.

Paul's mother and his three young brothers died in
Auschwitz. Judit, who was eighteen in 1944, died in Budapest
during an Allied bombing.

GOING HOME

The occupation of Hungary occurred swiftly. Within ten days every small town and village had seen German soldiers either on foot, in cars, or on motorcycles. The sight of their uniforms pulled my stomach into knots. Orders were out for Jews to wear a yellow star on the left side of their clothing. Not to wear one was very risky: being apprehended without the star drew severe punishment. How on earth was I going to make it home?

There were five students at the gymnasium in Debrecen whose parents lived in that part of the country where trains had to cross a major roadblock and be thoroughly searched. Jews who were taken off trains were never heard from again. Looking back on it, our plan to go home by train was a very simple and naive plan: the two boys traveling with us would be in the front of the cabin, casually talking to each other and would alert us when the Germans were coming. As two German soldiers approached, the boys kidded with them and pointed to us that we were their girlfriends. We held up some cards that looked like identification cards but without the religion stated on them. The soldiers barely glanced at them. In minutes the crisis was over.

I arrived in Szendro late at night. It was pitch dark. It was good that I knew my way around so well; every crooked stone and every hole in the ground was familiar to me. I became increasingly anxious as I approached our house. I knocked on my parent's bedroom window. They responded with apprehension. Though being with them instantly reduced the tension in my body, there was no complete relief; fear was the normal state of our minds.

I crawled into bed with my mother. She was shivering. Neither of my parents was sure I had done the right thing by coming home. This was a very small town—where would I hide? They thought of asking two of our neighbors to arrange a hiding place for me, but I didn't want to go into hiding; I wanted to stay with them. By now my brother Paul was in a forced labor camp and my younger brother, Andrew, was to leave soon. I did not want to hear about further separations. I just wanted the three of us to stay together.

I believe I slept for the next twenty-four hours. We all walked around as if in a daze. Little was said. We couldn't eat but used the outhouse frequently. The tension in our home, as in all Jewish homes, seemed unbearable at times. During the last few years, we had become accustomed to the shortages, especially in clothing and in kerosene. And we certainly had become accustomed to the severe anti-Semitism that had been the official policy of the Hungarian government for many years. Our response to the chronic humiliations was to consider ourselves superior to those who called us "dirty Jews." After all, who could claim as many Nobel Prize winners and could call themselves "the people of the book," as we could?

My father was exposed in our village to a particularly severe form of humiliation. In 1943, the heads of most of the Jewish households were arrested and interned. After they were released, they were put on house arrest and had to report to the police station once a week. They were made to wait for hours before an official would take notice of them, or they would be made to walk around the small yard. These elderly men were all punished for the same crime: being Jewish. Because my father was not permitted to travel, my mother had to take care of our store that was fifteen kilometers away.

At this time we were no longer concerned about the war-created shortages or about the many nasty manifestations of Hungarian anti-Semitism. We were now facing the prospect of deportation, a totally unpredictable future.

THE BACKPACK

Mother and I sat in the closed-in porch. This was the warmest and most pleasant place in the house at this time of year. The early spring sun streamed through the glass panels, playfully caressing the colorful stone-tiled floor common in houses of Central Europe. We sat close to the window, hoping the sun would loosen the stiffness in our backs and necks. But there was no escape from the tension that filled our bodies, that made us run to the outhouse with painful stomach cramps, and that kept our dry tongues glued to the roofs of our mouths. We worked in total silence, darning socks, knitting one more shawl and one more pair of gloves. The silence was broken from time to time by deep sighs that seemed to come from the bottomless fear that stayed with us day and night.

Only three weeks had passed since we listened to the rumble of motorcycles and heavy trucks as the German troops made their way through the village. They arrived at the end of March, and as the snow began to melt in the nearby mountains, the water was coming down in big gushes. The heavy equipment created deep grooves in the ankle-deep mud of the unpaved streets.

Now the streets were dry, and though the German soldiers moved on to the next town, the sunshine, the smell of the moist earth, and the sound of the birds returning to their nests were not in tune with our mood. Life in our house was winding down, not beginning anew. Paul was in a forced labor camp, my father was on house arrest, and we were now packing my younger brother's backpack, because he had received orders to leave for a forced labor camp.

How do you pack a backpack when you don't know where you are going and how long you will stay? This was spring, we thought, and he will need some light-weight clothes for summer, but the real danger to life will come in the winter. Snow and bitter cold comes early to Eastern Europe. He will need warm underwear, heavy boots, a winter coat, a sweater, a cap. How will all of this fit into a backpack, and how will he carry it all on his thin, small-framed body? Jews in forced labor camps had to march sometimes for days without a rest.

Mother was considered a master of packing. She used every inch available. As we packed and re-packed, we discussed what we could leave out and what he had to have. Could we put in some food, a piece of homemade bread maybe? My younger brother Andrew—Bandika, we called him—was twenty years old in 1944. He was a very thin boy. I still see him with his ribs sticking out when he was in his shorts or in a bathing suit. I see him walking in his slow, ponderous way, his shoulders slightly hunched forward—so different from the energetic, confident stride of my other brother, Paul.

Andrew was a handsome young man. Most striking were his large blue eyes set deep under his high forehead and dark brown brows. His mouth was prominent too; he had thick, sensuous lips, and just as in his eyes, there was always a touch of sadness around them. He was very serious about everything. We called him "the philosopher," always reading, thinking, arguing a point in history, politics or literature. He had told me that at age eleven I was not too young to read *War and Peace*, but he did not want to help me with a simple question in algebra because "how can you expect a girl to understand that?" He was three years my senior, and I thought him to be very wise and very knowledgeable.

As we packed and re-packed the backpack innumerable times, he kept trying it on, to see if he could lift it, if he could walk with it. We focused on how this skinny boy would be able to carry a backpack that was filled to its limit. It was good to be busy this way. While we were packing, he was still there, he was still with us.

Strange the way important moments in life become etched in one's mind. I don't remember saying good-bye to him, kissing or hugging him. I don't remember where my father was just then or what my mother looked like as she watched him walk out of the house. What I remember vividly is my own gaze fixed on the backpack as he walked through the door of the porch. I was watching intently to see whether the backpack was sitting tightly enough against his back, or whether the straps were cutting too deeply into his narrow shoulders. My preoccupation with the backpack dulled the pain of realization that we probably would never see each other again.

I found out in 1956 where and how Andrew died. I learned from friends that he died in Mauthausen, in a concentration camp, after the camp was liberated. Along with thousands of others, he died of typhoid fever, which swept through the camp just before the arrival of the American troops. His friends, who were with him when he died, spoke of him with affection. It was good to know that when he died they were with him, that he was not alone.

But how did he get to Mauthausen? Where was he between that spring day when he walked out of our home with his backpack carefully balanced on his shoulders and the day he died in a concentration camp a year later? I learned more about that in 1971, when I visited a cousin in Budapest. She told me that Andrew remained inside Hungary until late fall of 1944. When he found out that his unit would be sent out of the country, he planned to escape with my cousin's brother. The two boys were to meet in an apartment located inside one of the yellow star houses in Budapest. Andrew entered the apartment house after curfew and was spotted by the janitor who called the police. The two boys were picked up and taken away that night.

For her services, the janitor received thirty Hungarian pengos (about five dollars) from the authorities.

wheel

MOTHER

We called her "Mother." Not "Mommy" or "Mom" but "Mother,"
the way the peasant children called their mothers. My brothers
were in their "back-to-nature" mood when they decided to call
her that. During this time my brother Paul left the gymnasium
just before graduation in order to become an apprentice to a
plumber. An intellectual was considered to be a sissy; being a
proletarian offered more hope for survival. Calling our mother
the way peasant children did was in keeping with that spirit.

By 1944, it seemed that the war was going on forever.
Living in the country, where we raised our own chickens, baked
our own bread, and stuffed our own geese, we had enough to
eat, but everything else was scarce—especially clothing. Our
mother was concerned about keeping us warm and relatively
well clothed. Every girl and woman in the village was either
sewing or knitting. Whenever we would sit down, even for
relatively brief periods of time, we would reach for our knitting.
We knitted everything: sweaters, socks, gloves, even skirts and
dresses. Mother bought the wool directly from the farmers as
it came off the sheep, oily and dirty. The wool would be soaked
for days, and after it dried she would spin it into yarn.

After the occupation of Hungary, when various actions
on the part of the authorities indicated that deportation was
imminent, a sense of doom descended on every Jewish home.
Still, spring was spring, and I loved this time of year. The
village smelled new, especially in the mornings. The smell of
dew penetrated everything as it rose in the wake of the rising

sun. I woke early, enjoying the sound of the bells as the cows came down to the square to drink at the well. I could hear people coming and going, passing in front of our house. I recognized many by their footsteps. I listened to the noises: life starting up. Every morning held a new promise, especially spring mornings. For very brief moments, the tension would ease in my body, and I would indulge in a brief fantasy that the events of the last few weeks were nothing but a bad dream.

One morning, as I lay there, half awake, I heard the kitchen door open quietly. Mother must have gotten up early and gone out to the back porch. She loved to be on the porch, where the sun hit first in the morning. We ate our meals there in the summer, and mother liked to work at the long wooden table facing the yard, the barn, and the mountains in the distance.

This was earlier than usual for her to get up. I knew she must be very restless. Moving quietly, I went to the kitchen. The door to the porch was open: her image in the dawn of that spring morning has been with me ever since. She sat behind her spindle, slightly stooped. Deep lines furrowed her forehead, her eyes looking far into the distance. They were not focused on what she was doing, which was not unusual for Mother. Her hands were always busy, her mind always somewhere else. I looked at her hands: bony, narrow fingers, moving quickly. In her left hand she held the spindle head, twirling it with a speed that amazed me. I could feel the tension in her body. She was no longer agitated about the shortages, about the lack of money, or about the constant, oppressive news about the war. Her agitation was more excruciating than anything she may ever have felt before.

The feverish pushing of the pedal of the spinning wheel betrayed her deep concern, her fear, and the helpless rage she must have felt in the face of an approaching disaster. As I stood there watching her, I thought about her life. She lived through two cruel wars. In 1914, when World War I began, she was sixteen years old. I remember her telling us about the terror she felt when firing broke out as she was rushing to the home of her sister, whose husband was on the front. And now the terror was back: at age forty-six, her two beautiful sons were in forced labor camps and every day it was becoming more obvious that we all stood at the edge of an unknown abyss.

train

THE DEPARTURE

Six weeks after the Germans occupied Hungary, we were ordered to leave our homes. The Hungarian state police went from house to house, telling people they could take with them only the "bare necessities." What were bare necessities? Some underwear and a toothbrush? Could it include some family pictures? The house we were about to leave was designed by my father and had been the home of my grandparents, my uncle, aunt, their three children, and our own family.

In the chaos that followed the order, my ninety-six-year-old grandmother appeared to be the only one who remained calm. As we stepped outside the big iron gate, she looked back at the house. She seemed to have said something. Could she have been saying a prayer? Some kind of a good-bye? I only remember some words of reassurance—certainly no tears, no crying. She was a proud and very religious woman. The grandchildren helped her walk across the marketplace, down a narrow street to the house that was designated as the ghetto.

Our home was promptly taken over by the local police—their duties with the deportation of the Jews having been greatly extended. I shall never forget the reaction of Zombor, our big white watchdog, as we departed. The dog must have sensed that something extraordinary was happening. We were told that after we left, he curled under the bushes, remained motionless, and refused to accept food from his new owners. We had been in the ghetto for several days when a policeman came and took my father back to the house to feed the dog.

But Zombor refused to eat and lapsed into an irreversible depression. Emaciated and very weak, he was shot to death a few days before we were deported.

The ghetto for the forty Jewish families consisted of two or three houses. The beds and chairs were reserved for the older people, and the mothers gathered in the kitchen, trying to feed us, while we, the children, camped out in the yards. We lived on rumors: bad ones and good ones. One day, one of the young boys who had maneuvered our trip home from Debrecen asked me whether or not I believed the rumor that once we left the ghetto, we would all be killed. I answered with a quick "yes," though I doubt that I could truly accept that possibility. My answer shocked him. I was two years older, and he held me in high esteem; only a year before I had prepared him for his entrance examination into the gymnasium. He was the first one who told me about the possibility that we all would be killed. And indeed, he, his younger brother, and his parents became the victims of the Auschwitz gas chambers and crematoria.

We would have gladly accepted the conditions in the ghetto, horrible as they were, but we didn't stay there long. A few weeks later, in the first week of June, early in the morning, the state police arrived in full force. They were in their Sunday best: they had colorful feathers in their helmets that were secured with a chinstrap to their heads, not unlike the honor guards at Buckingham Palace. The shiny boots and the rifles on their shoulders gave them a particularly haughty and menacing appearance. They screamed their orders, pushed people with the butts of their rifles, and herded us into the yard of one of the ghetto houses.

The next thing that happened is very vivid in my mind.

I probably remember it so well because this was one of the most humiliating experiences of the many that were occurring those last few weeks in rapid succession. The men and women were separated, the women told to form a single line in front of a shed in which a midwife performed vaginal examinations on all women except the very young ones. That is where they expected Jewish women to hide gold and jewelry.

After being thoroughly searched, we were loaded onto several trucks—vehicles I had never seen in this village before. The only automobile in the village belonged to the doctor of the district, and it was never in running condition. Where did all these trucks come from? By now, the sun was up and the townspeople began to gather to watch this spectacle. With their arms folded, they looked on with bemused curiosity.

By the time we arrived at the train station a long freight train was waiting for us. The police—I had never seen so many of them before—were shouting and pushing people off the trucks. We were trying to hold onto our bundles and to each other's hands. There was no way of knowing what or who was on this train; all the wagons were sealed off, except two. The two hundred Jews of Szendro were then stuffed into the two empty wagons.

We were taken to Miskolc, only forty kilometers away. When we arrived, the whole train was unloaded onto the yard of a steel factory, a collection place for all the Jews in the area. Thousands of people were sitting on their bundles, talking, crying, looking for people they knew. In the yard of that steel factory I saw my mother's stepmother, my maternal grandmother, for the last time.

During the day, the place was in total chaos, but the

nights were remarkably quiet. I recall particularly well a clear, beautiful June night, full moon, very bright. The huge chimneys of the factory filled the air with smoke but not unpleasantly so. We were huddled in our blankets, and I felt snug and well protected lying between my parents. My father wept softly, and the three of us held hands. There was a strange sense of harmony and gratefulness in my heart: we were together. I even dared to hope that they would let us stay there. After all, this was the summer of '44. The Germans had suffered two horrible winters on the eastern front, and they were, we thought, losing the war.

Morning came and the dreams of hope vanished. There was much confusion when we were told that we would be taken back to the train station. People pushed and shoved and shouted as family members tried to find each other. They scattered their bundles, blankets, and suitcases after deciding not to carry them any further. Children cried as parents hurried them along. Young women carried old and sick people. There were no young men to be seen, because they had left for forced labor camps some time ago.

By the afternoon, things were quiet again. While sitting in the cattle wagon without room for our legs to stretch, the muffled panic we had been living with since March had overtaken us again. The air became suffocating. I believe I fainted several times. Someone said that a barrel in one of the corners of the wagon served as our toilet. But few people made it to the barrel. The wagon was too full to move around, and soon the air filled with the smell of vomit and feces. I found a spot near the corner of the wagon, next to my grandmother. As I sat near her, from time to time, she would put her hand on

my head and stroke my hair. It was growing dark, and as the
wheels of the train began to turn, people insisted on finding a
spot where they could sit down. In the general commotion, I
heard my grandmother saying her evening prayers. I would not
have dared to ask her then, but I would love to ask her now: did
she still believe that there was a God, that her prayers were still
being heard?

MARI NENI

She was a small woman. I see her coming toward our house with small, vigorous steps. She was always in a hurry. Seeing her was a joy in itself, because her presence meant fun, some good times that had become so rare in our lives.

As a young girl, Mari Neni was a maid in my grandmother's home. After she got married and her husband left for Canada to work in the mines so he could support his family, Mari Neni remained close to my father's family. I don't remember life without her. She was present at my birth, as she was present at the birth of all my cousins. I associate her small, wiry figure, dressed in the traditional style of the Hungarian peasant woman, with the most pleasant memories of my childhood. She helped us prepare for all our holidays. She took us out into the field when it was time to plant potatoes in the spring and harvest corn in the fall. Working in the fields was more fun than work for us. Though we were used to hard work, we did it only inside our homes, while time in the fields prompted fantasies of what life would be like once we got to Palestine.

During the years when our parents were preoccupied with the events of the war and the severe anti-Semitism, when our lives were deprived of the ordinary joys of everyday life and filled with the oppressive mood of anticipated tragedies, our Mari Neni—Aunt Mary—was there to bring joy and laughter into our lives.

Her courage and nobility were truly tested when we were

taken out of the ghetto and herded into the cattle wagons. As the heavy doors of the wagons shut behind us and as we tried to find a spot to sit or stand in a wagon that was filled with over a hundred people, I heard Mari Neni's voice. Gentiles were strictly forbidden to come to the station or in any way come near the train. But I heard her voice, calling my father. We could not see outside because the small windows providing us with air were located too high for anyone to see outside. My father managed to get close to where we heard her voice, and he picked me up so I could look out. And there she was! With her tear-streaked face, she strained to get a last glimpse of us and to wave good-bye. She must have been able to get around the police cordon by approaching the train through the fields. But the police noticed her anyway, and I saw her being subdued by two men as she raised her hand to her lips in a vain effort to throw us a kiss of good-bye.

I don't believe that I will ever forget this gesture. The rest of the townspeople showed us nothing but hostility, though they had known my parents and grandparents all their lives. They watched silently as we were driven to our final destiny. And here was Mari Neni with an open declaration of her convictions, with a rebellious expression of her feelings toward the family she loved. This makes her as much of a hero in my mind as any action that would have involved the use of arms.

I took our children to Szendro in 1971, so they could meet this extraordinary woman. She was seventy-two years old, her legs stiff with arthritis but her mind as bright and alert as ever. My heart beat in my throat in anticipation of this reunion. I opened the simple wooden gate to her small yard, which was full of flowers and vegetables—just as I remembered it. As she heard the gate open, she rushed toward us. Though with a cane, she moved with the same swiftness that I remembered from my childhood. We embraced, I kissed her tiny wrinkled face and let my tears flow. She felt my pain, my grief mixed with joy, and she, too, began to cry.

"Oh, oh, Annushka" she kept saying, "we have been waiting for you all morning, we weren't sure you would be here for lunch. But you are here and lunch is ready." She held my hand, stroked it, looked at me, and we cried.

Then she looked at the children: eighteen-year-old Sharone, thirteen-year-old Miriam, and eleven-year-old Rafael. She kissed them each in turn. Her joy at seeing them was extraordinary. She didn't speak English, and my children only understood a few Hungarian words, but their level of communication occurred on the highest possible human level. As she looked at them, her eyes filled with tears. I was sure she perceived herself the same way I perceived her at that moment: representing a past that we shared but of which now we were the only survivors. I believe she knew that I thought of her as a stand-in, not only for my grandmother, my aunts and uncles, but mainly for my father, who, she knew, had never seen my children.

We ate the lunch she prepared with the help of her daughter and neighbors. The meal could have been served by my own mother. From the chicken soup to the apple compote, these were all re-creations of my mother's tastes. I felt deep gratitude as I watched our children's delight in eating this meal. For them, the tastes of the soup and the apple compote established a sense of their own continuity. They were familiar with these tastes; they had grown up with them. Through this simple meal, the children could feel their grandmother's presence.

During the meal, and for a long time afterward, Mari Neni talked and talked as if she were under some kind of pressure to share with us everything she knew about my family. Every little detail mattered to her and she must have known how much these details mattered to me. She told me about my father's dream to become a doctor, his enrolling in medical school, but dropping out because he could not do the laboratory work in anatomy. The stories about my father were examples of his sensitivity and gentleness.

So, my father wanted to be a physician. What would it mean to him to know that his only surviving child, his only daughter he loved so much, had become one and that she is married to a physician and that one of his grandchildren had already fulfilled his dreams and the other two are on their way to doing so?

Mari Neni died in 1984. With her death, I lost the last member of my family.

figure

—

MY FATHER

When I think of my father, I first think of his hands. Father had soft, warm hands. When I was a little girl, I used to make a tight fist and bury my own small hands in his palm, so he could warm them up. It must be this memory that makes me think that his hands were soft and warm.

My father was a romantic, a very sentimental man; he was easily moved to tears. He was also a quiet man who emphasized good manners, proper behavior, and good language. It amazes me how much love for good books and good music our parents were able to communicate to us as we were growing up in that small village without electricity and without a public library. If anyone got hold of the latest Thomas Mann, Kafka, or Arthur Koestler, the book quickly made its rounds among the forty Jewish families. Hearing good music was more difficult. Without a radio or a record player, we learned to recognize the arias of some of the more famous operas from our parents humming them to us.

From the songs, I remember best my father's favorite, the song of Solvejg from *Peer Gynt*. The song is etched into my memory with the mood of a late Shabbat afternoon. It was dusk, too dark to read but not time yet to light the kerosene lamp and to say the Havdalah[1]. Father and I sat at the window, watching the cows come to the well for their long drink after a day of grazing in the meadows. As we sat, we sang this melancholy song about the aging and faithful mother patiently awaiting the return of her wayward son.

My father, romantic and sensitive, was a very bad businessman. The competitive, aggressive atmosphere of business life did not suit his temperament, especially during the war years when Jews could not get merchandise and could not get bank loans. Just before the Germans occupied the country in 1944, anti-Semitism reached a high pitch. Jewish homes were raided regularly, and the heads of families were arrested under all sorts of pretexts. My father eventually was placed under house arrest, and my mother took over the business.

Father loved nice things, nice furniture, nice clothing. When money was scarce and fabric hard to get, we spent weeks trying to decide on a material for a new suit for him. I still see him in a funny-colored green suit with pants shiny as a mirror but always sharply pressed. In the shabbiness of those war years, my father managed to look elegant. I think that elegance was in his hands, in those manicured fingers.

I was very protective of my father. He was fifteen years older than my mother, already forty-four when I was born. Because he was older than the fathers of my friends, I always worried about his dying. After all these years, I still have not fully accepted the truth about his death—that this gentle and quiet man had died in a shower that sprayed him with poisonous gas.

I last saw my father on the platform in Auschwitz. My memory is hazy about this. We all were semi-conscious from the long hot ride, but I recall that as the door of the wagon flew open, some strange-looking people in striped uniforms entered and began to throw our belongings onto the platform. The men, members of the Sonderkommando[2], were telling us that babies and children should be handed over to older people. The SS officers barked, "*Los, los, aussteigen, aussteigen!*"[3] became mixed with the screams of the children as they were torn out of their mother's arms.

My father and my grandmother were among the first to leave the train. I can still see him, holding onto his mother, putting his arms around her small, frail body. He was trying desperately to protect her from the crowd, but all around them people pushed and shoved in fear and bewilderment. I fixed my gaze on my father's back in hopes of not losing sight of him. But as the wagons disgorged thousands of people onto the platform, the crowd eventually separated us. The SS guards pushed people with their rifle-butts from both sides, and the crowd surged forward. As I searched for my father with my eyes and tried to catch up with him, I felt the firm grip of my mother's hand on my arm. I knew she and I had to stay together, that going after my father would only separate me from my mother too.

I saw my father one more time before the crowd swallowed him up completely.

I can only imagine what happened next. The tired, gray-haired man holding onto his aged mother appeared in front of Mengele. With a wave of his whip, he directed them to the left. For this pair, the verdict could only be one: death by Zyklon B. I don't know if they died together or not. My father was his mother's favorite son and he, in turn, was very devoted to her. I imagine that they held onto each other as long as they could. There ought to be some solace in that.

---

[1] Saturday evening service performed by lighting a specially braided colorful candle and smelling sweet herbs. The blessing over the candle bids the Shabbat good-bye and the sweet smell of the herb is to welcome the week ahead.

[2] Special units composed of Jewish inmates who were assigned to meet the transports and worked around the gas-chambers.

[3] "Hurry, hurry, get out, get out!"

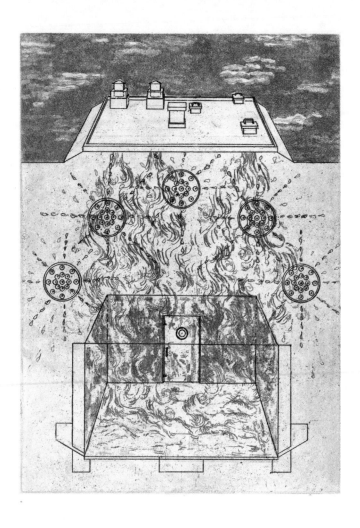

chamber

AUSCHWITZ: ANOTHER WORLD

Every time I think of the moment of arrival in Auschwitz, several images converge in my memory and become superimposed on each other. There is the image of my father disappearing in the crowd. There is the crowd itself, the frantic search for mothers, fathers, sisters and brothers, the little bundles people had been preparing for the trip sitting on the platform in a big, unruly pile. And there are the SS men and their dogs, the shouting, the barking, the commotion, the confusion, the panic. This was June, and it was daytime, but the air was gray and foul-smelling.

Mother held my hand. I was dazed. A column formed itself. There were constant shouts to hurry up. We kept moving. My twenty-four-year-old cousin, Margit, stood in line with us, but what happened to her mother and seven-year-old sister, Erzsike? We must have gone through selection, but I was not aware of it.

I don't remember when or where we were forced to undress. We were now naked and out of doors for what seemed to be a long time. Next, we sat on long benches, women in blue dresses standing behind us and cutting off our hair with long shears. The shears they used left our heads almost completely smooth. Our bodies were cleaned of every bit of hair: head, underarms, and pubic area.

"Radical Nakedness," author Terrence Des Pres called it. These are the best words for it; they capture the essence of the experience. To pass from civilization to extremity means to be shorn of the elaborate system of relationships, to lose one's social identity, one's family, all personal belongings, the entire cultural matrix that had previously sustained us.

The transition from civilization to extremity occurred within hours. We were herded into the next barn-like structure where clothing and shoes were piled up in huge stacks. We had to move fast, picking up the first item we could grab. Did the dress fit? What about the shoes? There was no time to decide. Whether or not the dress would fit was less important than whether or not the shoes we picked would fit. High-heels? Summer sandals? Shoes that were several sizes too big or too small? Picking a pair of appropriate shoes could spell the difference between life and death. Without socks, ill-fitting shoes would make marching impossible. They would break the skin and create blisters that could get infected.

After putting on a single piece of clothing, we formed a single line so that a wide red strip of oil paint could be put on the back of the dress. The significance of this paint must have been the same as the number that was sewn onto the front of our dresses, a way of keeping anyone from trying to escape from Auschwitz. Without underwear, our bodies were now protected from the elements by a single piece of clothing. But this was June. It was warm, and we could not think too far ahead.

"*Zu fuenf! Zu fuenf!*[1] shouted the women SS guards. These were the German words I heard most frequently in camp. We learned quickly to fall into line. Another column formed itself. We headed toward the interior of the camp and could now see better where we were. We could see the watchtowers, the barbed wires surrounding us, and barracks after barracks in endless rows.

At this time we were guarded by SS women, who kept us in the line. As we walked along I noticed a puddle on the side of the road and in a second I was out of the line, bending down, trying to wet my tongue. An SS guard promptly came after me, and I returned to the line before I fully realized the dangerous consequences of my actions.

We were herded into another barn-like structure. This was to be our living quarters, but there were no cots here. We sat on the dirt floor for several days, maybe for a week. The place was too crowded to stretch out our legs. We learned the first lesson of camp-life: survival required cooperation. We took turns leaning against each other's backs, trying to relax, trying to fall asleep.

They fed us some kind of cooked grass once a day. Tiny pieces of pebbles crunched between our teeth as we ate. When allowed, we ran to the latrines, which we needed frequently. A constant heaviness hung in the air—and a sweet smell too. I overheard mother telling someone that the smoke and the smell came from the burning of human flesh.

"Can that be true?" I asked her.

"Oh, no" she said. "That's just a rumor."

So my blessed ignorance remained relatively undisturbed. And blessed it was. It helped me to focus on the day-to-day, moment-by-moment events, something mother could not do. She was forty-six years old, and her energy was quickly disappearing. And the glasses she had worn all her life were taken away from her when we arrived in Auschwitz. I became my mother's eyes and hands, and she, in turn, used her brains for both of us.

---

[1] "To five! To five!" When colums were formed, we were put in groups of five.

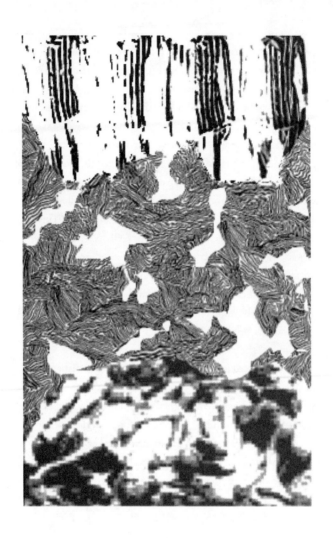

ballad

———

AUSCHWITZ BALLAD

By Margit F. Furth
Translated from Hungarian by Anna Brunn-Ornstein

The poet Margit Furth was my mother's sister. The ballad
is based on my mother's description of our experiences in
Auschwitz and other concentration camps. I have translated the
ballad so that our children—Sharone, Miriam, and Rafael—may
learn about their grandmother's spirit and determination.

I THE TRIP

Death,
there it lurked
and if you thought
you were a soul, a believer…
now guns will beat into you,
all you are is flesh and blood. Run
you wanderer!…
You've been thrown into
nothingness.

No sleep.
The wheels are turning
the train is shaking.
Eighty to a hundred
hearts, body and motor
locked in together.
This one is hungry
the other moans from pain…
and the fist comes down on you.
"A bit of water!" says the child.

Not a human anymore.
Guns, boots, revolver and
machine guns…
Only killing
what the crown of creation
has now on his mind.
And not whether you are
good or bad
rich, poor, a beggar or
an outcast,
it is the Jew in you that is the
victim of this torture.

One big heap of
body and bundles
melted together,
a small puddle
of water and vomit,
unconscious, fainting ---
and the cry to the sky:
where is God?

Summer country
shimmers outside.
Here it is dusk
thick saliva, perspiration, smell and dry throats,
"Oh, rain!"
says one reaching out through the tiny window
and all reach with
their cups…

Three-four
eight or ten days. Where to? How long yet?
between Hell and Heaven,
the train winds its way
on the border
between Being and Not-Being
the train winds its way…
it has no brakes.

II ARRIVAL

Gray fog
covers the horizon
---fresh air! A relief
Chimneys!?...A factory!?...
"Don't delay. Don't
look for your belongings,
get into a line!"
Everyone screams:
"You Jew!" You are alive...
only work awaits you?!

Women to this side!
Give their children to their
grandparents, quickly...Groups form.
Where shall you stand?
What will be "good"?
Your husband goes to the left
There...Selection!
The Mission?
...Ask the man in the uniform! He may understand
Don't be shy!

...it's impossible...
shall you hide? He shall look
at the masses...only at the heads.
On your head
quickly a red scarf. Young,
not a forced smile...Life
wants to live.
Into five!
...No noise...no commotion
Only the fog and the silence
outside. Inside the
thoughts can't find their places.
What's the smell?
Does it burn someplace?
And then the
Knowledge and the Terror combine...

III ONE NIGHT

Lambs...
They herd them and
cut their hair off...
Cut off hair
in a heap. According to color. Value!
The night falls,
naked, hungry bodies of women.
She watched:
will she get a wrap? Maybe a dress?

They herd them
into a corner
"No room for you here!
We have all that we can take."
What's the smell that
the wind is blowing?

Dark, silent night,
the wind pierces
into your bones
there is no cover...
You are condemned.
Say goodbye...pray...

Your heart is ice,
"Lean on my back
protect yourself and
don't ask questions
why–just hold onto my hand."
It is getting brighter now
morning is coming...
"Who is this? My child? Are you there?
Oh, my strength – my mind...
My sanity.....

Morning comes.
Selection. Pull out your chest!

What are you hiding with
your hands? Are you shy?
Your world had disappeared.
You don't see the end,
Only the whip. Hold onto yourself!
Beware!

IV AT WORK

Are you choosy?
It's too small for you?
Ill-fitting shoes
for you, Hungarians,
the last ones,
the curses, the beatings
it pounds and hurts in your
brain and in your face
as he comes down with
the heel of the shoe.

Food is from the pot
two pieces of potatoes. No underwear, no shirt,
you have no name.
You are not a machine nor an
animal. Numbers are tattooed into
your arm. Branded. A number.
A slave.

It's morning. Up!
Get up, can't be late, hurry.
The cold eats into you, you are trembling inside.
"Decimated were those
that were lazy. Does it pain you?
Into fives!...
...my child....! How will I save her...?

You lift the
stones with outstretched arms.
"Don't put them down!"
A shrill whistle pierces the air,
"Run with it!"
...the stones...the quarry...
....is he alive?
The whip comes down on
secret wounds,

it sinks into blisters, into sores.
The mud, the puss...
Care for it but it doesn't heal.
Be strong...there comes Mengele!
Hide! – Come out again...
The chimneys are smoking...
Something is burning...
Someone says,"garbage is burning
not the Jews..."
Don't believe it,
only think of the ghetto
loudspeakers were screaming:
"Who has a passport for travel?"

The crowd came.
Hope. – Will I be saved?
Then the train arrived ---
"Into the wagon! The soldier
kicks you and laughs
"Who had converted?"
Everyone runs for papers
still not understanding
the soldier's joke...
Someone screams..."Who is moaning?"

Oh, parents...
Give your children to
the German scientists. The
scientist is

doing his experiment…
It ennobles him.
He only takes pictures
makes movies;
he is human. – So you see – that's all ----

Waldsee….Fog
surrounds Auschwitz….
The motorized woman
like a torpedo shot out of
its hull
descends on the mother
and grabs the child
"Your baby!" And as if they were
kittens, no use to anyone
little bodies
dying in the basket
of a motorcycle…

They come to you
pictures upon pictures,
the fate of your sister
confronts you – now that her
fate is not in doubt.
Hallucinations,
spiders with thousand feet
coming out in the night
and the Kapos torture you. All you
ask for is a morsel….
…at least……!
you bargain With whom? With an
other and still an other thought.
Sanity stops here.
The fog, the gas and the barbed wire…
Who thought
you gain courage from beatings?...

Egypt.
The gray column
of slaves in tattered clothes
marching.
Strength comes out
of your very core....
When it comes,
but will it come?...The quiet
moment of death....

You tell me
about the one
the Doctor had "annihilated"
(torn to pieces...)
The infant...The lame...The old...
"Quiet, my sweetheart,
your mother is here.
There is God!"
....No....he too is gone....gone away.

72

V DEDICATION

Oh Dante...Heaven and Hell
Were created by the image of the
poet. The curse was boiling
in the cauldron...
....He too was thrown out – persecuted,
though he lived in a palace,
chiseling, shaping, forming
the past, the present and
the future
into a verse.

But, oh sister, this is not a play!
On your arm the tattoo
you recall it well!
this is not a poet's story
but created by the Devil. This
hell on earth.
Do souls suffer?
the living flesh had burnt. –
Sacrilegious are the rhymes,
the form.
Sister, I did not write to console you.

No, …No. This is not a Divine Comedy. Only
man calling to man; remember!

rock

———

IT ALSO HAPPENED
AT PITOM AND RAMSS

The summer of 1944 was hot and suffocating. We left
Auschwitz in cattle wagons much like the ones in which we
arrived. Once more we felt the uncertainty about where we
were heading. Once more we heard the monotonous drone
of the train. No water, no fresh air. But this time the trip
was short, only a few hours, perhaps. When the doors of the
wagons opened again, we looked out onto a dusty, treeless
hillside with long wooden barracks lined up in endless rows.
What kind of camp was this? What would we be doing here?
And where were we? Still in Poland? In Russia? In Germany?

The shrill voices of the SS women woke us from our
daze as we stumbled out of the wagons. "*Zu fuenf!*" they
shouted. They were everywhere. In tight-skirted khaki
uniforms, moving quickly, snapping their horsewhips, trying
to form a marching column from this group of bedraggled,
tired women. But we couldn't march. We could only drag
ourselves up the hill to the entrance of the camp. As we
shuffled along in our ill-fitting shoes, we whipped the
ankle-deep dust into a heavy smoke that burned our already
scorched lips and noses.

It was a short distance to the gate. Once we turned the
corner, we could see inside the camp. Not too far from the
rows of barracks we had seen from the train station below,
huge holes had been cut into the side of the hill. These were

stone quarries. The sight filled us with dread. From where we stood, we could see men in striped uniforms pulling loaded wheelbarrows. And again we could see the SS guards everywhere. This was a hill without a tree, without a blade of grass. It was all stone, gravel and dust.

Several hundred of us lined up in front of each barrack and after one more head count, we were permitted to enter. We ran for cots and grabbed the first ones we could put our hands on. My mother, my cousin, and I took cots not too far from the door. The horrid cots were made of widely spaced narrow strips of wood with a very thin straw sack on top. As usual, I slept on the top bunk of my mother's cot.

In the days that followed, we learned that the camp had been built on top of an old Jewish cemetery shortly after the German occupation of Poland. We also learned that we were in a place called Plashov, on the outskirts of Krakow, and the camp had a bad reputation because the camp commandant was famous for his cruelty. We saw him frequently, sitting tall and proud on his beautiful white horse with a horde of vicious dogs following him around. He would send one of the dogs after any prisoner he thought didn't work hard enough. We heard rumors that he had a Jewish mistress. We also heard that in the past prisoners had been decimated regularly at the morning "Appell."[1] Every morning, as we stood in the twilight waiting to be counted, I thought of the decimations. I tried to imagine what it was like to be picked to die—or what it was like for those who remained. We often reminded each other how lucky we were that those cruel days had passed.

We worked in the quarry every day. We picked stones

from one pile and carried them to another. The stones were not being used for anything. Nothing was being built here. We walked in a single line, snake-like, so that the SS women could see the size of the stone we carried. The stone had to be heavy enough to pull down our arms. My mother, who by now was very thin and weak, tried to pick smaller stones. For these attempts, the guards frequently beat her and sent back for a larger stone. I always managed to join her on these trips back. We did not dare to be separated, ever.

But our fate was not the worst one possible at this camp. Political prisoners, people from the Polish underground, worked the heaviest jobs in the quarry and were beaten regularly. Few men could stand up after such beatings.

We carried the stones in silence and dreamed about the thin soup and the piece of bread we would get at the end of the day. Sometimes we dared to dream bigger dreams, like sleeping in a bed with sheets, eating as much bread as we wanted, biting into a piece of fresh fruit.

In Plashov I stole food for the first and only time. We were standing in front of the kitchen, having finished our soup and gotten our bread for the next day, when an open truck pulled up loaded with fresh cabbage. When the truck stopped, a small head of cabbage fell out and began to roll down the hill. It took only a second for me to break out of line and run after it. As I returned to my mother carrying my booty, I saw terror in her eyes. For crimes like this, prisoners had been shot on the spot. We ate the cabbage right away, in a hurry. It would have been too risky to try to hide it.

We stayed in Plashov through the summer. Some time in the early fall, I believe it was September, they herded us back to the train station and locked us in cattle wagons again. Not too long after the train began to roll, one of the women peeked through the small window in the upper corner of the wagon and screamed with excitement, "We are in Vorsicht!" Mother knew what that meant. Since the woman didn't know German, she had mistaken the sign "*Vorsicht*" (Caution) for the name of a town. These signs were attached to the electric barbed wires surrounding Auschwitz.

Auschwitz meant selection. Auschwitz meant Mengele.

He stood on the platform in his high, shiny boots, looking into our faces, examining our bodies, assessing if we were able to carry on in a labor camp—or whether we were ready for the gas chamber. Mother put on her head a red scarf she found someplace in Plashov. By now, her shaven head exposed a very tired and aging face, which she hoped to conceal with the scarf. She was determined to get by Mengele again. And she did. With tremendous courage and with her hand firmly clasped around mine, we walked through once more, together, the Gates of Hell.

> [1] Appell was the head count, the most important event of the day. It usually occurred early, before sunrise, around 4:00 or 5:00 in the morning. We were awakened to the shrill sound of a whistle, climbed out of our cots, and went immediately to the yard, where we stood still in rows of five until we were counted.

camp

—

A NIGHT

Over the years fragments of a memory have crossed my mind, but I don't remember exactly when this event took place. It happened either shortly after we first arrived in Auschwitz or, more likely, during our second stay in the death camp. Only recently, with the help of friends who were with us at the time, was I able to put together the fragments.

It was late afternoon when we were ordered out of the barracks for a roll call. Several barracks must have been emptied at once because a long column formed. They counted us over and over again. Eventually the column began to move, and as the sun set we left the compound. While we crossed what looked like a highway, we saw several trucks and motorcycles. I remember one flat-back truck carried a stack of frozen, emaciated bodies. I still can see the long hair of women dangling from the tail end of the truck as it sped past us. After crossing the highway we found ourselves in an area we had never seen before. There were no barracks around here; an open field stretched before us and we could see the edge of a forest.

They ordered us to undress. By this time the sun had gone down, it became dark, and we were very, very cold. We were not permitted to sit or to lean against each other. The SS women kept up their vigil as they walked up and down, slashing the air with their horsewhips to keep us in line. Otherwise, all was quiet. We were completely gripped by terror. Mother looked for me frantically whenever I let go of her hand. Once, as I stood next to her, she asked me to leave because this was her

daughter's place. She may well have been delirious. Talking
was forbidden, but I knew that she could recognize me only
by my voice. My whispers eventually calmed her.

I don't know how long we stood outdoors—maybe for a
few hours; maybe we spent most of the night there. When the
column began to move again, we found ourselves in front of a
building. The lines that the SS women had tried to preserve
so carefully had broken up as people pushed and shoved to
get inside the building and out of the cold. I suddenly felt a
sharp pain in my back. As thousands of women were herded
into the building, I was pushed against the wall, my bare back
pressing against the rough surface of a wooden beam. The pain
must have awakened me from a stupor, and I could see better
the utter chaos and confusion going on around me. The crowd
separated me from my mother, and I was suddenly overcome by
panic. For a fraction of a second I thought that this may be the
end. Once the pain subsided, however, numbness and apathy
took over again.

Morning came. The guards ordered us out of the place.
They gave us some clothes and took us back to the barracks.
For years I wondered about that night. What had happened?

"Don't you remember the geraniums in front of that
building?" asked my friend years later. The geraniums were
placed in front of the "bath house" so that the people who
were taken there would think they would receive a nice
warm shower. I vaguely remember the geraniums. That
night was the closest that mother and I had come to a gas
chamber. Later, we heard that the constant flow of Hungarian
transports in the summer of 1944 had outstripped the
capacity of the gas chambers. Life and death depended on

numbers and simple logistics.

My memory of that night grew hazy in my mind because, I believe, I had never registered it fully. But it also is a night I have never completely forgotten.

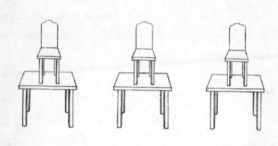

200
A-8-71

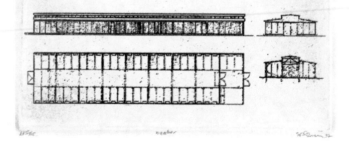

number

—

THE TATTOO

It was a brisk fall morning. Though the air was chilly, we could tell that it would be a "good day," dry and not too cold. We were told early in the morning—I believe during roll call—that we would be receiving tattoos that day. The announcement filled us with optimism. We thought that this was evidence that the Germans intended to keep us alive. We believed that receiving a tattoo meant that we would be sent out of Auschwitz again, perhaps to a labor camp, away from the crematoria.

This announcement came during our second stay in the death camp. The first time, only two or three months earlier, we were in a different part of the camp, in a more primitive unit.[1] During our first stay, our barracks seemed freshly built; they looked like barns, with dirt floors and no cots. We sat on the dirt floor at night, leaning against each other, trying to find a comfortable spot for our heads and backs so we could fall asleep. During the day, we were outdoors, again sitting in the dirt. How was it when it rained? I don't remember. The food, on the first stay in Auschwitz, tasted like cooked grass. We used the open latrines constantly.

Now, during the second stay in the death camp, we were in an older, more established unit. The huge barracks held more than a thousand women in each. We slept on cots, which were stacked three bunks high. The food was much better this time. We got our bread[2] every afternoon, which was to last through the next day, and a warm, thin soup every morning. We also got some marmalade with the bread once or twice a week; and on

Sundays there was stew made out of horsemeat, which tasted kind of sweet but not bad at all. Under these much improved conditions they told us about being tattooed.

I remember the weather having been dry and pleasant in the fall of 1944. The sun often kept us warm as we leaned against the outside wall of the barrack. Maybe because the sun kept us warm and for brief periods we were not being supervised, we dared to indulge in our favorite pastime: We would share memories from our school days, some happy or funny moments, the mischief we pulled on our good-natured professor who taught German language and literature. We also tried to remember the French songs we had learned in class just a year ago.

I wonder why I don't remember the rainy or windy days. In September or early October it must have been chilly, and we had no coats, underwear or socks in our ill-fitting shoes. On cool days we must have wrapped ourselves in our blankets that we were allowed to take outside.

We received the tattoo on a particularly brilliant day. They took us to another part of the camp sometime in the middle of the morning, and even from a distance we could see three or four tables standing in the middle of the road, with two uniformed girls sitting on the top of each of the tables. They looked very pretty to me. They had hair and were not skinny and dirty like us. Their navy-blue uniforms gave them status and importance. I believe they had some kind of emblem on the pocket of those uniforms. What could it have possibly signified? As we learned later, the girls were not German, but Jewish girls, fellow inmates from Czechoslovakia. They were a privileged class, well fed and well clothed. We formed long single lines in front of each girl.

Discipline must have been at a minimum. How else could I have roamed about to see which of the girls did the neatest job of tattooing? But I did just that, and I found "my girl." She was short, with dark hair and a friendly smile. I wanted my numbers to be small, well-shaped, and put on the inside of my arm. Most of the girls put on the tattoos sloppily, big numbers at a distance from each other, not in a straight line, and not on the inside, but carelessly on the outside of the forearm. When I got to my girl, I told her I had observed that she did the best job of tattooing. This comment obviously pleased her, and for my compliment she rewarded me with a small, neat-looking tattoo. I spoke German poorly at that time, but I tried to keep up a conversation with her. I very much wanted to be affirmed in my optimism, to be told that the tattoo meant that we would be kept alive.

We were disappointed when we learned the next day that the numbers tattooed on our arms would have to be done over. My original tattoo was B-71. The B signified that a new series of numbers would start with our unit. Instead, we were to be attached to an already existing A unit. My number now reads: A-B-20071. To my great relief, the numbers that were added to the previous ones were also small and neat.

We were proud of our tattoos, which gave us some sort of identity. We were not registered anywhere with our names, birthplaces, and ages. The numbers on our arms identified us, and we gave them added significance by thinking they would save us from extermination.

I'm no longer conscious of my tattoo but feel apologetic when I realize that it evokes unpleasant feelings in my friends. The tattoo reminds them of something they would rather forget. Whenever I see them looking at my arm, and I see their discomfort, I want to tell them that the day we received the tattoos was a good day for us, that we considered them to be "passports" to life.

People often ask me about my children's reactions to the tattoo. I don't believe they noticed it for a long time. To them, it was like a mole or a birthmark. Or could they have thought that all mothers were numbered? By the time they knew that I was not born with the tattoo, they also knew where and when I received it.

I recall a question our son Rafael asked me when he was about six years old: "Mother, are you sure you didn't do anything wrong when they did this to you?"

For a six year old, the world has to be just. Goodness should be rewarded, and only bad people should be punished.

---

[1]   A unit consisted of several huge barracks, each separated with electric barbed-wire fences from the next.

[2]   The daily ration was about seven ounces of dark, chewy bread.

THE SMELL OF THE PINE TREES

In the early fall the mornings were chilly. The days grew
shorter, though they could be warm. Whether this was still
September or October already, none of us knew. We had lost
track of time soon after we arrived in Auschwitz. On the
train rides from Szendro to Miskolc and from Miskolc to
Auschwitz, when the monotonous drone of the train lulled us
into semi-consciousness, the days and nights began to run into
each other.

Since our first arrival in Auschwitz, everything was an
approximation: about one week in the death camp the first time
around, six weeks or so working in the stone quarry in Plashov,
then back to Auschwitz and now, on this trip, we were leaving
the death-camp again. But how much time did we spend in
Auschwitz the second time? Six weeks or so? We thought Rosh
Hashanna and Yom Kippur had occurred during our second
stay there. Some thought they knew exactly when the holidays
actually occurred. We needed these days now more than ever,
but I don't think anybody really knew.

We left Auschwitz not knowing the direction or the
destination of the trip. We traveled again in closed cattle
wagons through countryside we couldn't see. When the train
stopped and the doors opened, we saw brilliant daylight
and more: we were in the mountains! We assumed we were
relatively high up, because there were fir trees all around us, and
we had felt the train climbing and winding its way just before
it stopped. The air was a bit sharp, very clear, and the smell of

trees almost intoxicating after days of smelling nothing but our own and other people's sweat and excrement.

As we tumbled out of the wagon and I set my eyes on the mountains, an immense joy filled me. I don't remember Mother with me. We always held hands, but I think I was alone for a moment. Where were we? What would they do with us here? These questions came not with fear but with incredulity. Could they really want us to live? This place could not be another extermination camp. There were no chimneys and not a trace of smoke. We could not see anything that looked like a factory. My bewilderment was interrupted by the barking of the SS women: "*Zu fuenf, schnell!*" Hungry and tired as we were, our steps had a bounce to them. We felt energetic in a way we had not felt in a long time.

90 | The march was short. We couldn't see the factory, but we did see some relatively low structures partly hidden behind the trees. This place must have been a winter ski resort in peacetime that had been converted into a factory during the war.

We were first taken to what looked like cottages set into the mountainside. Our joy truly was boundless when we discovered that a group of girls, dear friends from my hometown, were there. They told us that the factory was a textile mill and that the work was clean and relatively easy. We felt a sense of unreality. Were we dreaming? Given these circumstances, we would make it. Could we really be so lucky?

But soon confusion set in. Some people stayed in the cottages; others (like my mother, my cousin, and I) were sent outside to wait. We eventually were taken inside but not into one of the cottages. We were taken into a large barn-like

structure where we were to spend the night awaiting our
transport out of this dream spot. Even the Germans failed in
their calculations sometimes: more of us were taken to this
small mill than the place could accommodate. Ahead of us
stretched an anxiety-filled night. Would we be returned to
Auschwitz again, despite our tattoos, or would we be moved
to another labor camp? We immediately ceased to worry
about the fact that we could not stay in this little heaven; more
pressing anxieties took the place of such a frivolous concern.

The next day, an empty train arrived and picked up about
a hundred of us. We were taken to Parschnitz, another labor
camp a few hours away. After the war I learned that conditions
in the mountain mill were not nearly as idyllic as they appeared
to us that day. One of my dearest friends died there of some
kind of infectious disease, probably tuberculosis. We heard
that she was so severely debilitated that she could not fend off
mice that had settled into her cot and were chewing on her feet
before she died.

tower

———

THE BATH

The winter of 1944/45 was very cold in Europe. By the time we were brought to Parschnitz in the fall of 1944, we had lost a great deal of weight and were hungry all the time. We longed for the few hours of sleep at night, the only time we could forget our situation. But nights were a mixed blessing in concentration camps; falling asleep was not easy.

First, there were the hunger pains; we could not still the cramps in our stomachs. We received our daily bread ration along with soup as we entered the camp every night after work. The soup was a thin, warm liquid made with the chaff of various grains. We put the bread under our heads to keep it from being stolen. From time to time, I would be awakened by a piercing sound: someone discovered that her bread was gone. Once I heard a girl yelling at her mother: "Don't scream, you will die anyway, at least one of us will make it!" As I would lay there exhausted but unable to fall asleep, I would ponder, Should or shouldn't I bite into the bread? To take a bite was dangerous. I might not be able to stop eating and consume the whole piece at once, and then have nothing to eat until the end of the next day. We tried to save the bread and satisfy ourselves with the soup at the end of the day. Falling asleep without eating the bread was an accomplishment, and we made great efforts to achieve this victory over our growling stomachs.

Falling asleep was also difficult because the cots hardly had any straw on them and our bones kept hitting against the wooden slabs of the cot. But the worst part of the struggle, however, was fighting the bedbugs and the lice. Our cot was near the corner of a huge hall that at one time served as a factory. This spot gave us a bit more privacy than the ones in the middle of the hall and also more warmth, which may explain why large masses of bedbugs collected on the wall next to us. I still see them stuck together like grapes, hanging in the corner, right above our cot. As soon as we crawled under our coarse military blankets, the bugs attacked our emaciated bodies with a vengeance. Lice were a special problem for my mother. Without her glasses she could not see to pick them off from the little bit of hair that now began to grow under her arms, on her head and on the pubic area. How glad we were they cut off our hair in Auschwitz! Long hair would have been a nightmare without any opportunity to wash ourselves.

This is why I want to tell the story of how I got hold of some warm water and gave myself and my mother a bath from time to time. It happened one evening when I was, as so often before, preoccupied with the bread under my head. I was about to fall asleep when I heard water splashing, as if someone were taking a bath not far from our cot. I turned around and pulled myself up on my elbows to find the source of the sound. It seemed to be coming from the small area near the door, the only space that was not filled with double bunk cots and where a small light bulb over the door gave the dormitory a little bit of light. As I peered through the rows of cots, I could make out the faces of the camp cook and her girlfriend, the nurse. They were naked, washing themselves and each other with water from a pail placed between them. These two Polish-Jewish girls had been in

Parschnitz for many years. Since they did not go through
Auschwitz, they had hair on their heads and because they
had "positions" in the camp they had enough to eat: they had
full, round bodies. We all knew they were lovers; they hung
blankets around their bunk bed that offered them some
privacy. Rumor had it that they even had a sheet on their cot.

I watched them with envy, wondering if I should ask
them not to empty the pail after they finished their bath. I
could use the water to wash my mother and myself. I had to
move carefully. The girls were on the other side of the hall,
and I had to get to them without waking up my mother and
the others around me. It was important not to approach
the girls too soon, before they had finished, but not too
late either, when, in a second, the precious liquid could be
emptied into the toilet bowl.

My timing was perfect. I went up to the girls and told
them in broken German that I would love to use the water
and would put the empty pail wherever they wanted it. I was
afraid they would chase me away because I had come upon
them in this manner, especially since they both were naked.
But they were pleased that I had asked for the water and
promised to give their used water to me again.

I made my way back to my mother. I tried to wake her
up gently, because being awakened always meant bad news.
She startled, started to cry, and held onto me by putting her
arms around my neck like a child holding onto her mother.
Once she realized why I woke her, she was very pleased.
The water was lukewarm and looked gray in the dim light.
There was a rag in the water with which we washed ourselves
hurriedly. I don't remember how we dried ourselves, but

we felt refreshed. After all, this was the first time water had touched our bodies since we left home, at the beginning of June.

We kept our occasional bath a secret from the others, but I told my cousin about it. She was now a member of our "family," her mother and little sister having been selected for the gas chamber when we first arrived in Auschwitz. I made an effort to include her in everything that could make her feel less bitter and less envious. Very few girls had their mothers with them, and my cousin—seven years older than myself—was at times overcome with grief and envy as she watched Mother and I care for each other.

I believe that the luxury of our occasional bath played an important part in my mother's survival. She was now forty-six years old, and her skin was dry and brittle. An infection, starting with a small sore, could become a deadly disease. A bit of alertness, a bit of determination, and lots and lots of good luck had come together to make us winners in the constant gamble against the heavy odds that was life in a concentration camp.

bird

—

THE WINDOW

In Parschnitz, our lives came as close to ordinary prison life as was possible in a concentration camp. We were housed in a stone structure, and we got warm soup every morning and every night, a slice of bread for the day, and a cup of black liquid, called coffee, in the middle of the day. There were no random beatings in Parschnitz and selections for the gas chamber took place only in the infirmary. We followed our daily routine with a sense of resignation but not without moments of joy.

The whistle blew for reveille when it was still dark outside. We immediately ran to the bathroom, where the line formed quickly. I tried to keep a place for Mother, but the shoving usually prevented her from joining me. Using the toilet was a hit-and-miss affair.

It was still dark when we arrived at the courtyard for the head count. The SS women barked their commands to hurry up, to get into lines, and to form the columns for the march to the train station. During the march, talking to each other was strictly forbidden; the only sound we made was the click-clack of our shoes as we dragged our feet on the pavement. I don't recall seeing anyone on the street, nor do I remember seeing anyone at the train station. The townspeople must have boarded the train at some other place.

The trip to the town where we worked took less than an hour. In the yard of the factory the young and healthy-looking women were separated from the older ones. The young ones were taken inside the factory, and the older women were left outside to clean scraps of iron and wood from the yard. I dreaded this moment of separation from my mother, because I could not be sure whether or not I would see her again at the end of the day.

Entering the factory had many rewards. I loved the tingle in the tips of my fingers and toes as my body began to warm up. We went to our machines immediately. I worked with a large, complicated-looking monster that turned out some very insignificant-looking copper pieces that were supposed to be used in the building of airplanes. My job was to feed this machine with a strip of copper and to press on a foot pedal at the right moment, so that—without wasting any copper—I would get a perfectly shaped product. I had trouble reaching the foot pedal and remained in constant fear of letting the cutting edge of the machine come down on my fingers. I heard stories of people cutting off their fingers with this machine when their coordination failed them. Still, I liked my machine; it had "status," and it kept me indoors.

The overseer was an old German factory worker. He rarely spoke to us. The only time I remember him standing at the door of the factory and "greeting" us was when news reached Germany that President Roosevelt had died. He was eager to tell us about this and did so with a sardonic smile. We dismissed the news as German propaganda. SS women supervised our conduct and our work, enforcing the rule of not talking even more strictly inside the factory than on the street. Our guards walked between the machines and stopped from time to time to check on us. We had permission to leave our work area to go to the bathroom twice a day—once in the morning and once in the afternoon.

We planned our brief vacations away from the machines with care, because we could exchange a few words with our friends in the bathroom. While standing in line we tried to recover the lines of a poem or piece together the plot of a favorite novel. My mother was very helpful in these mental games. Because she used to read widely, she could fill in details that would make a poem or the plot of a novel more complete.

Making two trips a day to the bathroom, having a noon-break for "coffee" (some funny-smelling black fluid), made the days in the factory tolerable. With the coffee came the piece of bread we had saved from the day before. We drank a sip of coffee with each bite of bread to make the bread last longer and fill our stomachs better.

But the afternoons could be very long. Hunger preoccupied us all the time, and as the day wore on, fatigue made handling the machine increasingly more difficult. As the sun began to set and the whistle blew, we moved quickly to the yard, where I looked for my mother so that we could march back to the train station together. We were not permitted to talk to each other on the train either. By this time, however, we didn't feel like talking. Our minds were focused on the soup we would receive when we got back to camp.

And I had something else to look forward to: I had a fantasy that I savored and indulged in on our way from the factory to the camp. The fantasy focused on a window that belonged to a small house in Parschnitz. The house faced the street that took us back to the camp, and every night I looked forward to seeing it. My attention was drawn to the window because of the curtains, which were white and were pulled to the sides, framing the window in the shape of a soft V. The roof of the house came down in a sharp angle, common in one-family homes in Central Europe. The window was directly under the eaves of the roof. The small room I imagined behind the window must have been snugly tucked under the roof. I had an elaborate fantasy about the room. It had a highly polished wooden floor with some simple homemade rugs. The narrow bed, which was directly under the eaves, had clean sheets with the faint smell of soap. It had a pillow and a down cover. Next to the bed sat the night table with a small lamp and books piled on it, and I placed a larger and much brighter lamp shone on the writing desk that stood in front of the window. Clean underwear, warm sweaters and wool socks filled the chest of drawers. Tiny red, blue, and yellow flowers covered the white wallpaper. In the spring, I put geraniums in the window. In the winter, a small bird feeder sat on the windowsill.

102

I saved the fantasy for the march back to the camp, as if I could permit myself to enter the room only when my window came into sight. Putting myself into that warm little space made the labor of walking in someone else's shoes, being hungry and totally exhausted, just a little bit easier to bear. But I also remember thinking how unlikely it was that I would ever have such a luxurious place.

Once inside the camp, as we stood in line for the spoonful of thin soup, the fantasy died. It could not survive the pushing, the shoving, the noise, the hunger, and the cold. We passed the window every day, and, as if I were in love, I looked forward to seeing the window again. I waited anxiously for those few precious moments, when I could transport myself into a clean, warm and friendly place.

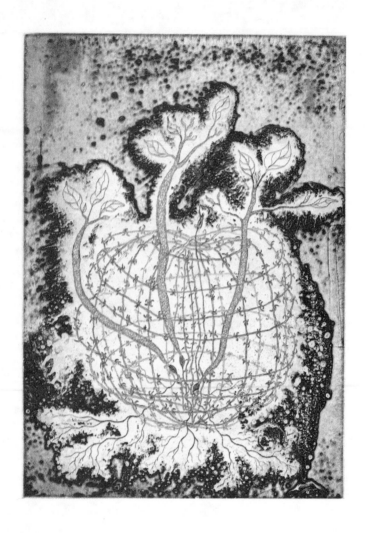

world

—

THE CORE OF AN APPLE

We had gone to the infirmary earlier that winter, when Mother developed a painful, pus-swollen sore on one of her ankles. We had a hard time deciding whether or not she should go, because the Germans used the infirmary to select women for the gas chambers, especially women who were considered incurable. For a woman her age, being in the infirmary meant almost certain death. But at the infirmary, with some luck, we could get ointment to heal the wound, which otherwise was sure to become more infected, making her selection unavoidable. We were lucky: Mother got some ointment and a piece of cotton that she could place between the sore and her shoe. She was sent back to work, which was important.

Her work, however, was cruel. It was intended to slowly kill a group of middle-aged women. She was part of the clean-up brigade, the "*Putzkommando*." These women were constantly out of doors, collecting and cleaning rusty scraps of metal that were scattered in the factory yard. Without warm clothing, without underwear, they were not only exposed to the wind and cold but also to cuts and infections, the most dreaded complications of camp life. Mother did remarkably well under these conditions, and so we were worried and scared when, later that winter, *I* was the one who became ill.

We had heard rumors of typhoid fever in the camp. When my stools became watery, and I felt weak and faint, we knew I had to go to the infirmary, whether I feared it or not. I don't remember actually going there. I must have become comatose.

I do remember the physical set-up of the infirmary and some
of the people there. I recall the huge outer hall with lines of
cots and bunk beds, and the nurse's station at the end of the
hall. I remember most vividly the tiny, closet-size cubicle that
I shared with another young girl who had tuberculosis. She
was the daughter of a famous rabbi and—in an effort to save
her from selections—she was hidden there for over a year. She
slept in the bottom bunk, and I slept in the top. We tried to
communicate in German mixed with Yiddish.

I don t know why I was taken into this privileged spot.
In retrospect, I think it might have been because of my
appearance. Without hair, and being small and skinny, I looked
very young. I recall many people who were kind to me in
Parschnitz. Of all the people who were kind, I remember best
the nurse at the infirmary. She was a red-haired, middle-aged
woman who was feared by everyone, because it was her job
to take the SS doctors to the bedsides of the women whom
she considered "incurable." These women were sent back to
Auschwitz to be gassed. Parschnitz was a labor camp and did
not have facilities for extermination. But this very same woman
was hiding me from the possibility of a selection. These were
the riddles of camp life!

I witnessed only one selection in the infirmary. One night
I saw two SS officers come in and flash their lights as they
pulled the covers off the women. The women must have been
too scared to scream. It was a quick, matter-of-fact procedure.
When I began to feel better and was no longer at risk to be sent
back to Auschwitz, I was moved into the big hall.

Mother came to the infirmary almost every night. I looked

forward to the few minutes of her visits. I worried about her a great deal, because she looked very skinny and was tired all the time. I knew I was getting better because my diarrhea had stopped and I was very hungry again. When Mother came, we talked about the rumors she had heard about the war. We were very discouraged when rumor had it that Budapest was still under German occupation. This was January 1945, close to my eighteenth birthday

But more often than not, we talked about food. I remember telling her that it was strange that this time I was thinking less about homemade bread and more about fresh fruit. I kept thinking about apples and tomatoes, promising myself never to slice them again as I wanted so badly to bite into one. These were foolish fantasies! We were in the middle of a cold winter and in the middle of what felt like an endless war.

But miracles do happen. Somehow my mother found the core of an apple. She found it, I believe, on the street close to camp, on the way back from the train we took every day to the factory. She saved the core of the apple for my birthday. And what a present it was! There were a few good bites left on the core. I wanted her to share it with me, but she insisted that it was my birthday, and so I ate it all.

I still love apples more than any other kind of fruit. My family often teases me about how I eat an apple with such obvious relish and how I always eat it completely. No part of it ever gets thrown away. What my family may not realize is that I am looking forward to eating the core, that I love the core the best. Eating it always raises my spirits and renews my belief in miracles.

THE DAY OF LIBERATION:
MAY 8TH, 1945

The day before had been unusual. We had not gone out to work and had not gotten anything to eat. Something definitely was going on. There were rumors that the end of the war might be near. Some people heard that the Allies had thrown down leaflets from airplanes about the war being over. Our excitement was mixed with fear: would we make it or would the end of this nightmare come some other way?

The routine of our prison life had drastically changed in the last twenty-four hours. This became even more obvious when I woke up and found the sun up; the first time in a year that I had missed the sunrise. We had been awakened every morning when it was still dark outside, but today there had been no reveille. The huge hall with its five hundred women prisoners was quiet. Why was everyone still asleep? I made my way to the window, which looked onto the courtyard. From the second floor of this old factory building, the view from the window went beyond the camp boundaries. I could see the street and the edge of the forest beyond. I was terribly apprehensive as I looked down and made out the figure of the lager commando; he stood next to a horse, his car parked on the other side of the yard in front of the living quarters of our jailers, the SS men and women. Now, for the first time, I noticed that the gate to the courtyard was wide open, that there was no sentry! In my bewilderment and excitement, I let out a scream that brought the other women to the window. In total disbelief we watched the commando mounting his horse while nervously tearing the insignia from his uniform. We saw him racing out of the yard toward the forest. We saw him disappear! Now the realization was complete: I had just witnessed part of the German defeat; a German on the run! This indeed was the end of the war!

When I turned around to get back to my cot, I could not move because the crowd of women who gathered at the window kept pushing me against it. If the windowpane, which reached from the floor to the ceiling, would break, none of us could survive the fall. Taking a chance of being trampled on, I tried to crawl back to my cot between the women's legs.

By the time I made my way back to my mother, the huge dormitory was in utter chaos: sounds of Polish, Yiddish and Hungarian mixed together as the women cried and screamed all at once. We all wanted to get out but were paralyzed by the sense of uncertainty. My mother, too, was frightened and bewildered. Was this the way a war was supposed to end? The overwhelming joy of having lived to see the day of our liberation was mixed with fear: what would happen next?

In my daydreams, I had skipped this moment. I had often imagined myself free, and in my mind I would indulge myself with huge quantities of homemade bread. But how would I get there? What happens when you actually become free again? I was in a daze. I held onto my mother's hand, and we decided to leave the building. We went down to the courtyard, which was by now swarming with the two thousand women of this single building. Everybody was pushing, trying to make their way to the pantry. With its doors wide open, we could see what was inside: sacks filled with flour, sugar and beans. I was shoved along with the crowd and got separated from my mother. The temptation to dig into this stuff was tremendous. As I was about to reach for the sugar and could feel its taste in my mouth, I heard my mother scream at me: "Don't touch it! It could kill you!" I felt like a two year old who had just been scolded and knows she has done wrong. I could have taken a can of the cold beef lined up on the shelf, but I knew it was best to get out of there as soon as possible.

The rest of the day was spent in continued chaos and uncertainty. Some of the Polish girls got hold of two SS women who had not been able to get away. They cut their hair and dunked their faces into the overflowing toilet bowls. Conditions inside the building deteriorated rapidly. The two bathrooms were overused and broke down; thin, foul-smelling feces trickled down the steps. If we were lucky to have survived the Germans, we now had to find ways to survive our freedom.

Many of the women ventured into the town. They begged for food or some of the more enterprising ones started to loot. But most of us remained on the grounds, sitting in the dust, hoping that someone would come and tell us what to do. Where did we get the piece of red cloth that we used as a Russian flag? We hung the cloth on the gate, hoping to welcome our liberators. Mother and I were sitting close to the gate when we saw the first Russian soldier—a single messenger on a motorcycle—arrive late in the afternoon. He was covered with dust, hoarse with exhaustion. He stopped his motorcycle and asked for a table to stand on so he could speak to all of us. He spoke in Yiddish. What he said was not encouraging. He was here to "officially" liberate us, but he did not promise any help, telling us we ought to fend for ourselves. He told us that he had liberated many camps that day, and the Russian army was in no condition to provide transportation or to feed us.

With the departure of the Russian soldier, the chaos and uncertainty increased. We were in a panic. Small groups formed. Everybody had to find her own solution. We were driven by hunger and fear. We spent about a week in Parschnitz trying to figure out what to do. During the day, we knocked on the doors of friendly Czechs asking for food. They were friendly, but because of the way we looked, they could not let us into their homes. They dug a hole in the yard and kept a large kettle of potatoes boiling there. We ate the potatoes with salt and drank water from the well. Meat, butter, and milk were at a high premium. These Czech farms had been thoroughly plundered by the withdrawing German army. At night, we slept out of doors in constant fear of being molested by Russian soldiers, many of whom had not seen a woman for years.

While under these chaotic circumstances we heard that Czech and Slovak girls would be able to go home because trucks were arriving soon to pick them up. My mother suggested we declare ourselves to be Hungarian-speaking Slovaks, because we lived only fifteen kilometers from the border, a distance, we easily could walk. I balked. I did not want to lie. I insisted that if we had been able to live through our imprisonment without lying, I would not do so at this time. Mother begged me to listen to reason, but I was adamant.

My honesty could have cost us our lives. The Hungarians were not interested in bringing back their Jews to Hungary. We had to find our way. A week later, nearly fifty of us left Parschnitz on foot. We did not know exactly where we were or what direction we should start walking. We had no plan for getting food or finding a place to sleep. The journey was much more difficult than we could have anticipated. We spent our days looking for food and some place where we could sleep without the danger of Russian soldiers finding us.

And we had not anticipated the many physical obstacles in our way. One day we came upon a wide river but couldn't find a bridge. When we found one it was halfway submerged in the water. The river looked shallow there. We crossed it by climbing the wreckage and found ourselves in a small, bombed-out village. There was no one in sight. We saw some hungry-looking dogs and a couple of goats climbing from one heap of rubble to the other. This was an area where a great deal of fighting must have gone on, something we had not witnessed in Parschnitz. In areas where people had not yet returned to their homes we usually found an abandoned house with some potatoes in the cellar, and we took shelter for the night. Fortunately, we made this journey in May, and most days were dry and relatively warm.

Gradually as we were able to fill our stomachs we began to worry about whom we would find alive once we made our way home. We had no way of knowing that the news awaiting us would be harder to bear than anything we had endured in the course of the past year.

A DECISION

It was a beautiful day, sometime at the end of May or early June in 1945. There was a gentle breeze blowing across the small hill where Mother and I were sitting. In front of us stretched a track of land, leaving the view open to the mountain range far in the distance. It was quiet, unusually so. The other women—there were about fifty of us trying to go back to Hungary on foot—were somewhere in the nearby woods, looking for anything edible, but the berries were still green on the bushes.

The night before, as we searched for a place to take shelter, we spotted on top of a hill an L-shaped building that looked like a school. The Germans often used this kind of building for their troops, and we hoped we could find potatoes there and spend the night. Indeed, the basement of the building was filled with potatoes, buried in dark soil, which was the customary way of preserving potatoes for the winter in Europe. There were bunk beds with straw sacks and blankets on the first floor: a luxury hotel! After a good night's sleep, Mother and I boiled the potatoes. We found a big pot, dug a hole in the ground, gathered some wood, and started a fire. I don't remember how we started the fire. We must have found some matches.

That morning I stretched out on the hillside, basking in the sun, enjoying the breeze and the quiet of the place. With the quiet and the prospect of food came a sense of contentment and hope. Mother, too, looked relaxed. For the first time in a long time we spoke about home. The smell of the fire and the crisp, fresh air reminded us of those early fall days when we cooked prune marmalade in our backyard for the winter. The weather also reminded us of the preparation for Passover: putting away the everyday dishes and bringing down the Passover dishes from the attic.

I loved those pre-Holiday preparations! I loved the extra care we took to clean the house. Father was not supposed to find any breadcrumbs when he went around, looking into corners with his feather brush. I had the impression that this was some kind of a game, a pretense, that father knew he would find no breadcrumbs. But tradition had it that, at the end of the search, the wooden spoon and the feather brush had to be burnt. We were still reminiscing when suddenly I turned to Mother and told her that if Ornstein Pali were alive, I would marry him. I knew why this thought came to me with such clarity and certainty just then. The thought of marrying Paul made me feel very safe and very secure. I was convinced that he would make all fears and uncertainties about the future disappear in my life. I felt warm and good inside: all new sensations in my eighteen-year-old body. Strange, though, I never considered that he may not want to marry me.

We heard the other women coming up the hill. The scene changed immediately. We were hungry, and the potatoes weren't ready to eat. We also had to make a decision about what to do next and in what direction we ought to be heading. Feelings of uncertainty led to arguments, and people threatened to split off from the group. The noise and the apprehension about our future washed away the serenity and the contentment of the moments before.

We stayed in that place for another day, because
we couldn't leave the potatoes behind. Walking became
increasingly difficult, and some days we seemed to be going
around in circles. We walked along railroad tracks that helped
us to get from one town to the next. We were hoping to get on
a train, but with most of the tracks bombed and destroyed, our
chances of finding a train were not good.

Then, one day, we heard a rumble.

I don't remember how or where the train stopped to
pick us up. Our excitement mixed with fear when we realized
that the train was filled with shouting, boisterous soldiers.
We feared the Russian soldiers; the stories about their raping
escapades were vivid in our minds. But these were not Russian
soldiers. They were Yugoslav partisans heading back home
to Zagreb. The train had to go through Budapest, and the
commandant in charge offered to take us along. This officer
ordered his men to empty one of the wagons for us. Soon they
brought us some stew. All of these events seemed a bit unreal
to us.

As soon as the train started to move again, we fell
asleep and woke up only when the train came to a sudden
stop. We now were inside Hungary. The station had a
Hungarian name. It was a small station, with only a few
people hanging around, and Mother and I got off the train
to get some fresh air. A young man walked next to the train,
looking into faces, calling out names, searching for someone
he might know.

Then something extraordinary happened. As he came
close to us he looked into my mother's face and asked if
she were related to Brunn Pali. Yes, Mother said, she was his

mother. The man, with considerable excitement and conviction, told us that he had seen my brother after the liberation in Rumania, that he was sure my brother was alive, and that he probably was home by now.

Deciding that our search had to begin somewhere, we agreed to go to my aunt's apartment in Budapest, without knowing whether or not she or any other member of the family would be there. As we walked down the wide boulevard, people stared at our hairless heads, at our tattered clothing with the camp numbers clearly visible on them. We walked in complete silence, not daring to utter the questions that had been on our minds ever since the liberation: Who will be alive? Did anybody from our family come back?

Standing in front of my aunt's apartment, I felt paralyzed and could barely ring the bell. I felt a sense of relief when my aunt came to the door. The expression on her face gave the answer to our unspoken questions, as the flash of excitement and joy upon seeing us was quickly replaced by a shadow moving across her face. We understood the meaning of her changed mood: only we had returned. Until now, nobody from our family had come back. Did my aunt have any news about the boys? Was there any word about my father? These questions could not be asked yet, because we were not ready to hear her answers. The questions remained unarticulated, hanging in the air, too urgent, too important, to be spoken out loud.

From that moment on, my memory is hazy. I believe I slept for several days. From time to time, I opened my eyes only to fall back to sleep. I was in this somnambulant state when one day, as I opened my eyes, I saw his breeches. I knew right away that they belonged to Ornstein Pali. He bent down to kiss me, and I hugged him—a wordless affirmation of a decision I made a few weeks earlier.

THE RETURN

In 1945, Budapest was a bombed-out, hungry city. Food was rationed—not only meat, butter, bread, and milk, but vegetables too. It was my job to get up early in the morning and stand in line for some of the vegetables that had begun to reach the city.

During the first few weeks after our return, we lived in my aunt's small apartment. Living with my aunt was the right thing for my mother. The two of them were soul-mates. Mother talked, my aunt listened. My aunt was a poet, and not long after our arrival, she wrote one of her most powerful poems, which I have translated from Hungarian into English. Her "Auschwitz Ballad" is a testimony to my mother's ability to observe and describe, and my aunt's ability to listen and understand.

During the war years and for some time before that, my aunt's small apartment was a meeting place for writers, poets, and all those whose political views no longer could be discussed in public places. Her oldest son was an ardent Zionist. He had left Hungary at the age of eighteen and helped start a left-wing kibbutz in Palestine. Her second son was an equally ardent Communist. In my aunt's small apartment, he made plans to join, along with his friends, the civil war in Spain against Franco in 1936. When Ornstein Pali lived in Budapest, attending school there, he frequently joined the Friday night gatherings, and he was inspired by the intellectual vigor and strength of commitment with which political and literary issues were discussed.

As much as Mother and I enjoyed living with my aunt, we could not stay there too long. We had to move on, to begin our lives again. The question of my going to work never came up, because I had to finish high school first. The Jewish gymnasium in Budapest prepared to open its doors in the fall of 1945, and I had a great deal of catching up to do.

Before beginning my studies, however, I had to prove that I attended the gymnasium in Debrecen for almost two years. As I sat in the waiting area outside the director's office, I was very apprehensive, wondering what if my words would not be enough. Where would I find someone who could testify that I had attended the gymnasium in Debrecen? When the door opened, I immediately recognized that this was the same man who was director of the school in Debrecen when I was a student there. More importantly, he also recognized me. Before I could say anything, he came to me with out-stretched arms.

119

"You are one of our children," he said. "One of our children has come back!" He embraced me and held me as if, indeed, he had just found one of his own children. This behavior was typical of those days. We constantly searched people's faces, hoping to recognize someone we knew before the occupation. Finding someone gave us the sense that our destroyed world could be at least partially restored. We spoke briefly about our respective experiences during the last year. He gave me an outline of the courses I was expected to take, and I was on my way. I had to find someone who could help me with Latin and all the subjects in which I was not strong.

My tutor, a dear friend of my mother, lived in an apartment building near the Danube—an area of the city that had been exposed to heavy bombings. All the windows in the apartments were blown out. I would arrive early in the morning and would crawl immediately into bed with her, the only place one could keep reasonably warm. The blankets she had hung on the window frames kept out the wind, but the apartments had not been heated for some time. Keeping warm was even a more challenging task than finding food to relieve one's hunger.

We spent about an hour every morning studying Latin and ancient history. I was eager to learn, she was eager to teach, and I made excellent progress with her. After a few months study, when I took the required examination for admission, a lady from the interior ministry came to the school and gave a special mention to my achievement in Latin. This recognition gave my confidence a boost. I was back on "track," and once more I could focus on things other than sheer survival.

Not long after my mother and I returned to Hungary, Paul's father came back from Mauthausen. He was totally emaciated, nothing but skin and bones, his skin yellow because of a severe case of hepatitis. Paul was determined to "fatten" up his father and me. He could not achieve this goal in Budapest, but food was more plentiful in Rumania, so he decided to take his father and me to Cluj, where he first attended medical school.

There were no passenger trains between Budapest and Cluj in 1945. We had to get onto a freight train that made slow progress, which would not have been a problem except for the constant rain. I remember crouching in the corner of the open wagon, Paul and his father standing next to me, trying to shield me from the rain and wind.

The trip was worthwhile. There was plenty of milk in Rumania and plenty of cornmeal, the country's national staple food. Paul also bought some colorful blue and red fabric, which we took back to Budapest so Mother could make a skirt for me. She also made a blouse from a pillowcase. In these clothes I felt very elegant.

But clothing remained a problem. For my wedding, I wore an off-white wool suit and a beret that belonged to my cousin. The only thing that was new and belonged to me was a pair of brown walking shoes that had to be good for everyday wear. Paul wore a suit that had belonged to my brother, a suit that Mary Neni had hidden along with other small items, all of which she returned to me.

Our wedding was beautiful. But that is another story.

IMA AND HER FORTY CHILDREN

They were skinny and sad-eyed. They had lice in their hair. Their skin was dry and bruised. We expected them to be hungry all the time and to eat well. Instead, each child had one or two favorites and asked for the same food at each meal. Through food they tried to stay in touch with their past, with what was familiar. Mother wished they would eat the fresh fruits and vegetables she worked so hard to get for them, but she had to take her cues from the children.

This was an orphanage for forty Jewish children, ages four to thirteen, whose parents did not return from the camps or wherever they may have been during the occupation. The children had been hidden by Gentile families and now, with the end of the war, they came to the Jewish agency. Some of them had spent the last few days of the city's siege in the sewers.

Mother was in charge of the orphanage, located in a lovely villa in the outskirts of Budapest. She insisted that all the other caretakers take the same attitude toward the children that she took, meaning that the orphanage should not be an institution but a home. To gain each child's trust and make him or her feel safe had priority over everything else.

The children rarely asked about their parents or referred to their lives before the occupation. Perhaps we may have been the ones reluctant to ask such questions of them. They had nightmares, for sure, and many struggled to fall asleep. Every adult in the house became part of the nighttime routine. Mother wanted all adults—the cook, the gardener, the maid, whoever else was around—to stay with a child who had trouble falling asleep.

To provide individual care for forty children was an extraordinary task. One of the most time-consuming and difficult jobs was cleaning the girls' hair. We treated their hair with some unpleasant-smelling liquid in the evening, and washed their hair every morning. The dead lice had to be removed with combs or by hand. Their hair was long, but Mother did not want to consider cutting it. Our own hair had not yet grown to full length, and she found the idea of cutting the little girls' hair totally unacceptable.

The children were not ready to attend public school, so they had their own school and a wonderful teacher in the villa. Snacks and outdoor activities frequently interrupted the hours spent in school. Mother made spending time out of doors another priority. The villa, a spacious, lovely house with well-kept grounds, proved to be an ideal setting for these children.

With the physical and relative emotional recovery of the children, came Mother's own recovery. She put on weight, and color returned to her face. I noticed most of all the return of her smile and the shine in her eyes, especially when she was with the children. She put amazing energy into planning their meals, supervising the cook, the maid, the gardener, and she had long discussions with the teacher, who became her friend and closest collaborator.

In March 1946, Paul and I got married under the chupa that was set up in the garden of the villa. The ceremony took place on a Wednesday afternoon. We made the decision to marry that particular day on Monday, only two days earlier. We picked that day because Mother had a nice-sized hen and could prepare the traditional "golden soup" for the occasion.

Few people attended our wedding: Paul's father, one of his uncles, and the relatives who survived the war in Budapest.

After the chupa and the meal, Mother opened the door to the study adjacent to the dining room, where she had arranged the children, standing on chairs and benches, into a small choir. Each child held a lighted candle. As they sang their well-rehearsed Hebrew and Hungarian songs, their faces glowed in the candlelight with joy and excitement.

My young husband turned out to be exactly the way I imagined him on the day I decided to marry him: he was energetic and decisive. The Hungarian Communist regime became more oppressive with every passing day. Paul believed we had to leave the country and escape into Western Europe. We hoped that as refugees we could go to Switzerland and study medicine. I struggled with this decision, knowing that mother would not leave the children, but Paul was adamant about leaving.

Three weeks after our wedding, we tried to escape from Communist Hungary into that part of Austria that was occupied by the Western Allies. These illegal border crossings were organized by a Zionist underground movement that helped surviving Jews escape from Eastern to Western Europe. We were caught on our first try but succeeded the second time. After a brief stay in Vienna, we made our way to Bavaria into a Displaced Persons Camp and eventually to Heidelberg where we began our medical studies.

Our escape separated mother and me for two years. During those two years, she managed to smuggle most of the children from the orphanage into Palestine. Because of her connection with the Zionist underground, her stay in Hungary had become extremely dangerous. One night in the spring of 1948, responding to an urgent tip indicating she was facing immediate arrest, she left Hungary. By then, however, the iron curtain was in place, successfully separating East and West. Her escape through the minefields was much more risky than our journey out of Hungary two years earlier. By 1948, Paul and I lived in Heidelberg, studying medicine at the university. Mother joined us there, and once more she became Ima (mother) to more than her only surviving child. She prepared the noon meals for all the Jewish students, most of them Holocaust survivors, who came to study at the University of Heidelberg.

First, the young orphans in Hungary, and now the homeless students without families in Germany, could appreciate her care, her cooking, and her attention. Being called "Ima" by so many, and with such affection, was medicine for her.

There were to be two more years of separation. As refugees, Paul and I had to leave Germany for the United States when our numbers for immigration came up. This occurred in 1951. Mother could not get an entry visa to the United States for two more years. She still lived in Germany when I wrote to her that we were expecting our first child. She received the news with extraordinary joy. She had hoped for such news. Now she really could be a mother again. Sharone, our oldest child, was six months old when my mother joined us in the US. She immediately took over the baby's care, as she did Miriam's four years later, and very briefly, two years later, Rafael's too.

As I watched her bathing, feeding my children, reading them stories, putting them to bed, and taking them for walks, I thought at times that the love and pride she felt for them—and the pride and joy she found in the children of our friends—could help her overcome the immense grief of having lost her own two sons. But now I know that such grief does not diminish with time.

Learning about her sons' deaths was the most brutal emotional pain my mother had to endure. Until her own death, sixteen years later, Mother and I rarely spoke about my brothers and made only rare references to my father. She kept her unspeakable grief to herself. We would have felt selfish and indulgent to speak about personal losses when everyone around us suffered similar fates. People were envious of us, because we had each other. Very few women my mother's age came out of Auschwitz twice as she did and survived the many selections we had gone through while we were being transported from one camp to another. We could never forget that we were very fortunate to have survived together, that we were among the lucky ones.

Mother died in 1961, at the age of sixty-three. She is the only member of my family with a burial place. Mourning her and the others in my family has been a life-long process. Feeling the pain of their loss keeps them with me, forever.

GIVING THANKS

This was the time of day Mother loved best. It was the middle of the afternoon, just after the baby woke from her nap. The child stirred, babbled a bit, and reached up to her grandmother. This moment had become precious to my mother. Day after day, she sat next to the crib, waiting for the baby to give the familiar gurgle. She picked up the child, held the small body tight and the child, half asleep, leaned her head against her grandmother's chest. Sensing the little body going limp in her arms, Mother nestled the child's head into the nook of her shoulder. The moist warmth of the head against her bare skin soothed her aging body. But just before she became totally relaxed, she put down the child and began to prepare for their afternoon walk.

With the little girl securely tucked in a blanket against the chill of the late fall day, Mother walked the quiet, suburban streets with a steady gait. In the last two years, since she had come to America, she had become familiar with every house and every garden in this stately neighborhood. She stopped from time to time and looked at the leaves that covered the ground, trying to identify the tree a leaf may have fallen from. She tried to keep her mind busy, focused on what was in front of her, what was in the present. She had to be very careful about that. There was always the danger that a thought or a fragment of a memory would twist her stomach into a painful knot and she would start bleeding again. That had to be prevented by all means.

The streets were empty. Nobody was out walking at this time of day. The wind became stronger, and the air felt colder. From one of the yards, there came the scent of burning leaves. This smell made her sick to her stomach, and she felt slightly faint. The acrid smell transported her to the top of a garbage heap, and her nostrils filled with the odor of slow-burning rubbish. She could see the women in their rags, her teenaged daughter among them, turning over the tightly packed city refuse layer by layer, just as the SS guards told them to do. The work was easier than carrying stones in the quarry, but the smell of slow-burning garbage seemed to have stuck in her nostrils forever.

To escape the repugnant odor, Mother quickened her pace. The carriage began to bounce as it rolled down a small incline, and the baby laughed with joy. When the carriage finally slowed down, the baby grinned at her grandmother, a smile that brought back the happiness Mother only recently had begun to feel again.

At night, when the house was quiet and her eyes grew tired from reading, she knew that her little tricks would not work. The piercing ache in her stomach signaled that she could no longer avoid thinking about the fate of her two sons. At first, she thought of the good times, when the boys were small and she was a young woman full of hope and expectation for their futures. Her sons were close in age, barely two years apart, and were healthy, lively youngsters, the older strong willed like she was, the younger quiet, more like his father. Raising them in a small Hungarian village was difficult, but she managed and was proud of the way she took care of her family in those trying times.

Rousing herself from this risky illusion, Mother turned on the light. She began to read a new book by James Michener, *The Source*. The book took her into ancient times, far away from the horror of the big war that took away her most cherished possessions.

Mother was always an avid reader. In America she wanted to get acquainted with the best in English literature. When not busy taking care of our children and preparing meals, she read or listened to the radio; the news, she knew, affected people in their daily lives. Just the other day, we were listening to a program about all the things we ought to be grateful for. This reminded us of the end of the war, the day of our liberation when we were filled with hope that the war we had just survived would be the last one mankind would ever have to witness. How fervently we wished for peace! And now, here we were, nations were making bigger and better weapons and were killing each other in higher and higher numbers than ever before. Why do we continue to live in the shadow of wars all the time? We all long for peace, for families to be together, to celebrate life together, to bare the pain of illness and death together. Since the first trainloads rolled into Auschwitz and Treblinka, there have been other large-scale killings in the world. The Holocaust was not necessarily the end but it might have been the beginning of an era.

It was important not to give in to these thoughts. She had to be strong. Over the years, we both learned how to create a feeling of safety when the world around us was in turmoil. Mother turned her thoughts to the joys of setting a beautiful table, lighting the fire in the fireplace, making the house inviting and comfortable. She will soon hear the bell ring and the

But she could not keep her thoughts from wond[er]
the darkest period of her life, when money and food b[e]
scarce, when rumors coming out of Vienna, Prague, an[d]
Warsaw became more and more scary, when she first sto[p]
sleeping through the night because of a deep dread that [her]
beautiful sons might be taken away from her. Now, ten y[ears]
after that cruel war ended, she still could not be sure wha[t]
happened to her oldest child, a handsome, blue-eyed boy, n[ot]
yet twenty-two when she last said goodbye to him.

There could be no doubt about the fate of her husband [he]
was sixty-one years old at the time of deportation to Auschw[itz]
and could not escape the fate that awaited a man his age in a
death camp. She had recently learned the fate of her younger
son, twenty-year-old Andrew; she knew that his frail body
could not survive the starvation and the horrible conditions in
a forced labor camp. The day she heard about the death-march
that took him to Mauthausen, the most dreaded camp in
Austria, when she heard that he died a day after the camp was
liberated, had become the day of his funeral. The separation
from her younger son had become final, but the pain of having
lost him, no less.

But what about the older boy, Paul? Was he not the strong
and resourceful one? Everybody said that if anyone would
survive the war, it would be him. She only knew that the forced
labor camp in which he served was attached to a Hungarian
military unit that was stationed on the eastern front. Was he
dead or could he still be alive? She found herself indulging in
the faint but persistent hope that her first born, the one so
close to her heart, was alive somewhere in Russia, that vast and
impenetrable country.

Hornsteins, who have become our extended family, will arrive
and the house will be filled with the noise of the most precious
sound of all: the sound of happy children playing.

Tomorrow, she thought, her daughter, the youngest of her
children who survived several camps with her, will take her
shopping. They will buy a good-sized turkey and she will cook
everything the way they do it in America.

Mother loved Thanksgiving. Where did this holiday
originate? How did it get started? She thought that to
set aside a day to reflect on one's good fortune was meant
especially for those who knew that this country—with all its
shortcomings—is the best country in the world. Tomorrow,
she will have to look into the encyclopedia, find out the details.
Exhausted, she turned off the light. Settling her head into
the comfort of her pillow, she pulled the soft blanket over her
shoulders. With tension easing in her body, she finally fell
asleep, thinking about cranberries and sweet potato, wondering
why in Hungary they did not grow such magnificent food.

My mother lived in this country she admired and loved
so much for only eight years. During her final illness, her
granddaughters, Sharone and Miriam, "took care" of her,
and she learned English from them and with them. She was
delighted to witness the birth of our youngest child, Rafael; he
was one year old when she died.

THE MISSING TOMBSTONE

Judith, or Jutka, as she was called, was two years my husband's junior. Because she was the only girl among four boys, she was very special to her parents and to her brothers.

I did not know Jutka. We had only one brief meeting. I know that her father adored her, that her older brother thinks she was "a sweet, warm, extremely good-natured girl with a great many intellectual interests." He also tells me that Jutka had long, wavy brown hair, white skin, big brown eyes and full, sensuous lips. She had a limber body and loved to perform little stunts. Because of her love for gymnastics, she took dancing lessons and was an accomplished soloist at high school dance recitals.

In 1943, Jutka moved to Budapest to study dental technology—not an uncommon profession for Jewish girls, who were barred from higher education. She lived in a home with other Jewish girls, who were studying in the big city and whose families lived in the countryside.

Three month after the Germans occupied Hungary, Jutka's mother and three younger brothers were deported to Auschwitz, while her father and brother Paul went to a forced labor camp. I often wondered how she felt to know that her mother and younger brothers were taken away and that her father and older brother were out of the country. I imagined that she must have lived in constant fear for their lives. I was wrong about that. Not long after the German occupation, heavy bombings of the city began to occur day and night.

Budapest was under siege from the fall of 1944 until its liberation in January 1945. The girls in this home had no idea where their families had been taken, but the constant threat to their own lives obliterated any concern for others. They could not have known that while they listened to the blare of the sirens or ran to the shelters their families, after being collected into ghettos, were deported to extermination camps.

The house where the girls lived was designated as "a yellow star house," where only Jews could live. Every morning, the occupants of the house, escorted by two Hungarian soldiers, marched out of the house to clean the streets from the previous night's bombings. The girls had to sort, clean, and stack fallen bricks. One of the women would start a fire on a make-shift grill and cook the meat from the horses killed in the previous night's bombings. One time they were lucky indeed. They came upon a whole sack of dried yellow peas. From then on they ate yellow peas every day—a sustenance for those who had difficulty swallowing the horsemeat.

Other than during this clean-up, the occupants of the houses could go out only between two and three in the afternoon and only with the escort of a Hungarian soldier. They were supposed to do their "shopping," except there was nothing to buy at that time of the day. The small amount of fresh vegetables that found their way into the city all were sold in the morning. Bread was rationed. Everybody received about ten ounces of bread, which the girls usually ate in the morning with some thin liquid, called coffee.

Sometime in September, on the eve of one of the high holidays, the sirens went off again, and the girls ran down to the shelter. Because she had twisted her ankle, Judith could not run fast, but she managed to keep up and was not left behind. As the bombs fell, the twenty-four girls and their teacher sat together in one corner of the shelter that suffered a direct hit. As they started to run into the adjacent room, the ceiling above them fell in, and the teacher, along with five of the girls, among them Judith, were killed instantly.

The survivors made their way into the shelter of the next house. When they emerged, they could not recognize the street. They saw only rubble and dust. They watched as workers pulled the bodies from the obliterated house. Soon six bodies were laid out on top of the rubble. The woman who related these events to me said she remembers noticing that the watch on the teacher's wrist was still running. They buried Jutka in the Jewish cemetery in Budapest.

134 Years later, Paul and I stood in the middle of this large, relatively well-kept cemetery. We very much wanted to see her grave, to spend time thinking of her, remembering her exuberant, lively personality. But we could not find the grave. Why was it so important to us to find her grave? We knew she was not in that small heap of earth, that she was in our hearts, and in our minds where her memory could not easily fade. But we persisted and with the help of a map and a cemetery worker, we located the grave, which was completely covered with weeds and heavy overgrowth. We could not find the tombstone. Paul looked crest-fallen. We wanted to see the stone, but we wanted even more to see her name written on the stone. We now realized that this is why we came. We did not want to think that she, too, was in an unmarked grave in an unknown site, like the rest of our siblings.

Why do families visit gravesites? Why do they sometimes

read the names on them out loud? I've seen pictures of visitors to the Vietnam Memorial in Washington: the fingers lovingly stroking each letter of the name, the camera focusing on the face of the griever, who shows a mixture of sorrow and a strange calm—a calm accompanying a moment of intense grief.

We visit gravesites because we want to remember. And we want to remember because only those who are forgotten are truly dead. The man who cleared the grave from the overgrowth offered to arrange for a new stone. We feel better knowing that there is a simple stone that reads:

ORNSTEIN   JUDITH,   1926-1944.
HER MEMORY SHALL BE BLESSED.

THE SHOVEL

I didn't think I would ever want to go back to Auschwitz to
see what the place really looked like. The decision to go came
to us slowly. Our plan was to go to Hungary, travel through
Czechoslovakia, and spend some time in Zakopene, a resort
on the Polish side of the Carpathian Mountains. Paul wanted
to visit the part of the mountain he crossed during the bitterly
cold winter of 1944, when he was escaping from the forced
labor camp. During his journey, he wore a pair of badly torn
pants, and suffered constant hunger as well as fear that he
would be captured and killed.

When we returned, we traveled in a nice big car and stayed
in resorts where only the very rich could stay when we were
children. After we crossed the Czech-Polish border, it made
sense to visit Krakow, a medieval city with a magnificent town
square and churches from the twelfth and thirteenth century.
And can you be in Krakow and not go to Auschwitz, which is
only seventy kilometers away?

Before we set out to the death camp, I wanted to find
the stone quarry in Plashov, near Krakow, where Mother and
I worked in the summer of 1944. This was a difficult task,
especially since we do not speak Polish, and we could not find
anyone who could speak either English or German. We drove
up and down a highway, trying to find a sign that would put
us on the right track. I was ready to give up when, suddenly,
and almost simultaneously, we spotted a hill with a jagged,
unnatural-looking outline. We drove around to find access to

the place. As we drove closer, I grew more convinced we had found the right spot. We eventually came face to face with a gravel yard, and I could see the excavation reaching deep into the bowel of the hill. This was the pit, the graveyard where thousands of Jews and political prisoners died.

I found the man in charge. We had language problems, but once I showed him my tattoo he cried out, "*Zydowka! Zydowka!*"[1] He knew exactly what I wanted to see. With gestures and lots of excited sounds, he confirmed that this, indeed, was the stone quarry where Jews worked and died during the war. He wanted to take us to see the barracks or some houses where the barracks used to be, but it was almost noon and we wanted to go to Auschwitz the same day.

On the ride to Auschwitz we passed through beautiful countryside, peasants tending the fields, horses and cows grazing peacefully. Auschwitz was actually in this world; it was surrounded by ordinary human life! That eerie, otherworldly image I carried with me for almost forty years did not fit what I was now seeing. During the trip I spoke almost uninterruptedly. It was very important for me to talk, to relate my first trip to Auschwitz to the two young people who were riding with us in the car, a pair we were giving a ride from Krakow to Auschwitz.

Before this trip, I had not realized that Auschwitz consisted of two camps. Auschwitz I was not an extermination camp. This camp has brick buildings that were built during WW I for prisoners of war. During WW II, it housed Jews and political prisoners who worked in nearby factories. Birkenau (Auschwitz II) is about three kilometers from Auschwitz I and is a very different place. There were no brick structures in Birkenau. The prisoners lived in huge wooden structures, built like barns, but most of these wooden barracks had been destroyed. The chimneys left standing appeared to be reaching to heaven in a silent but persistent scream.

In Auschwitz I, there is a small crematorium that was used during the First World War. I could touch the items that were used for this gruesome job. In front of the gaping mouth of the oven was a narrow shovel, maybe ten inches wide, placed on a narrow, rail-like contraption. The function of the shovel was obvious: to carry the dead bodies into the oven. I stared at the shovel. How could a human body, the body of a grown man, be placed on this? With all the evidence of horror around me, it was strange that I should feel the deepest sense of indignation and be most deeply affected by the sight of this shovel.

The image of the shovel has stayed with me, and since then I have often reflected on its meaning to me. In our civilization, we treat the dead with special reverence. We separate from their bodies slowly, over time. We arrange for funerals, listen to speeches that extol their virtues, hold memorial services, and observe mourning periods. Fixating my eyes on the shovel, as if mesmerized by it, may well have been a brief memorial service I held for my father. I thought of him during the entire stay in Auschwitz.

Whenever I think back on the image of the shovel and feel the full force of my rage and indignation, I think of Simon Wiesenthal's beautiful book *The Sunflower*. Every day on his way to a forced labor camp, Wiesenthal passed a military cemetery where a sunflower was planted on the grave of each soldier. He imagined that the sunflowers gathered up the rays of the sun, and by carrying these rays to the cold earth, warmed the bodies of the dead soldiers. As a Jew, Wiesenthal could only expect

138

to perish, should he become sick. And as a Jew, he could only anticipate being tossed into a mass grave after he died. None of his dear ones would know when and where he died.

I do know where and when my father died, but I have a hard time accepting *the way* he died.

[1] Polish word for a Jewish woman.

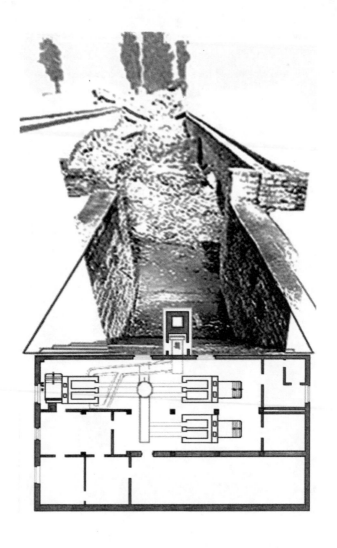

steps

———

"THE STEPS MY MOTHER
DID NOT WALK DOWN ON"

The trip from Krakow to Auschwitz took less than two
hours. In the car with me were Sharone, our oldest child, her
husband Jeff, who drove the rented car, and Miriam, our second
daughter, pregnant with her first baby, Adina. We missed
our son Rafael and his wife Susannah, who was at the end of
her pregnancy expecting their first child. Sharone and Jeff's
two sons, nine-year-old Zachary and seven-year-old Noah,
remained with their grandfather in Krakow, not ready for this
trip at their age.

    We left early in the morning knowing that one day
is not quite enough to see both camps, Auschwitz I and
Birkenau (Auschwitz II). We were eager for this trip but also
apprehensive about it. I was concerned that I would not be a
good guide for my children, but in Auschwitz I, we did not
need a guide. The red brick buildings now serve as a museum
with good English descriptions. These barracks originally were
built for Russian prisoners during World War I and housed
Jewish and political prisoners who worked in the nearby IG
Farben in World War II. To see the pictures of some of the
individual prisoners on the walls, to read the documents, to see
the punishment cells where the prisoners had no room to sit but
had to die of hunger and exhaustion, to see the barracks where
the sterilizations and other human experimentations were
conducted, to see the brick wall against which the prisoners

were executed, to look at and experience the impact of the mounds of hair, baby carriages, artificial limbs, eyeglasses, empty cyanide canisters and suitcases, and to go into the barrack reserved for Jewish visitors where the El Maale Rachamim is playing continuously, all of these could have taken a whole day or more.

A punishment barrack in Auschwitz? Think of the irony: in a place where there are six gas chambers only three kilometers away, there is a courtroom where "hearings" were held. A judge sat at a table and meted out sentences for "special crimes." The difference between dying in the gas chamber and dying in Auschwitz I was that death in the chambers came with relative swiftness, but here the prisoners had to suffer before they were allowed to die.

142 | In Auschwitz I we saw the model of the gas showers. It detailed the process whereby the masses were moved from the area where they got undressed all the way to the "elevators" that delivered them to the ovens. But the Germans ran into a problem: people could be killed faster than their bodies could be disposed. This fact slowed down the process. The solution was to burn the bodies in open pits; the heavy smoke and the sweet smell that hung over Birkenau did not come only from the chimneys. The number of people killed in Birkenau can only be approximated from the number of empty cyanide canisters that were found here: about four million.

As I am writing this recollection I hear people wonder: do we need to know these details? I don't know, but I think that not knowing is a bad idea. In *The Plague*, Camus wrote: "Plague is not made to man's measure, and so we tell ourselves that plague is unreal—a bad dream that will pass. But the dream does not always pass, it is people who pass, humanists especially, from bad dream to bad dream, for they were not careful enough."

It was early afternoon when we started to walk the dusty, treeless grounds of Birkenau. It was hot but none of us seemed to mind. We wanted to see everything; every little detail mattered to us. I hoped I would remember some details that I did not properly register when we first arrived in Birkenau in June 1944. I had a clearer memory of the place when we returned there in the fall of the same year.

We started our pilgrimage at the watchtower behind the entrance gate. From the watchtower we could look down at the endless rows of tall chimneys, the only structures that remained from the wooden barracks that were destroyed when the camp was turned into a museum. The sight was eerie, unreal and my eyes (my mind?) could not encompass it all. There is a map at the entrance with the description of the various barracks: barracks for the Gypsies, for the homosexuals and a special barrack for the Czech Jews brought here from Terezin, where families were kept together for propaganda purposes. After their arrival, they were told to write letters to relatives in America and Australia saying that they were fine and treated well. After their letters were collected, they all were gassed.

Of the thousands of barracks the camp once contained, only a few were left standing, many of them part of B block, where I believe my mother and I were housed on our second stay in Birkenau. We walked into several of these barracks; the first two looked unfamiliar. This bothered me. I could not remember our barrack having had indoor latrines; we did not have anything quite as luxurious as that. Later in the B block, I found a barrack that looked exactly the way I remembered it;

the whole length of the barrack was stacked high with three-tiered bunk beds. What I did not remember was just how narrow the area was in front of the bunk beds. There was no place to stand even for a minute. No wonder that after we were awakened (I'll never forget the shrill whistle of the guards), we had to go out of doors immediately regardless of the weather, fall into lines of five and stand for roll call for hours. I don't remember getting anything to eat or to drink in the morning. I do remember staying out of doors all day. We did not work in Birkenau. Every morning, after the roll call that served as a selection, some people were taken to the gas chamber or shipped to one of the labor camps or remained in Birkenau until their fate was decided depending upon their physical condition.

144

So, how did we spend our days in Birkenau? Years later, on a visit to Israel, I met Chaja, the lovely redhead my mother took under her wings. She asked, "Do you remember how your mother helped us recite poems by Ady, the famous Hungarian poet? Just think, Ady in Auschwitz! And do you remember when your mother found a piece of red rag? How happy she was that she could cover up the gray stubs of hair that began to grow on her head?" I remembered the red rag but not that my mother was concerned about the gray stubs of hair. I was happy that Chaja remembered the incident that represented my mother's resourcefulness and her unwavering capacity to remain in touch with the cruel reality of Auschwitz.

It was on this trip with our children that I learned about the capriciousness of my mother's and my own survival. I overheard a guide talking about an area at the far end of this ghost city, an area called Mexico, which served as a "holding

station" for Hungarian Jews. I now understood why we were
in barracks without floors and without bunk beds when we
first arrived in Birkenau. We were so tightly packed that we
could not stretch out our legs; we sat on the dirt floor and
took turns leaning against each other's backs to get some rest.
I remembered the cooked grass with pebbles in it that we got
to eat and how I kept running to the latrines. The barracks
were next to the gas chambers, next to the forest that hid the
crematoria. The forest, too, was a holding area. A sign now
informs the visitor that this was the area where whole families
were kept waiting for hours, sometimes for days, to enter "the
showers." Here stood (or sat if they could find place) mothers
with their crying and hungry babies, grandparents trying to
keep their tired and frightened grandchildren quiet, most of
them not suspecting what was awaiting them. We moved on,
but the image of the forest and the eerie silence of the place will
always be with me. Can anyone imagine the agony these trees
had witnessed?

We did not think we could possibly see anything more
distressing, but we had not yet seen the pits where the ashes
from the crematoria were collected. Somehow, Miriam and I
got separated from Sharone and Jeff. It was getting late in the
afternoon and Miriam was getting tired and the sights had
become increasingly difficult to bear. We stood in front of the
pits filled with ashes and groundwater. In front of these burial
places stood small "tombstones" with Polish, English, German,
Hebrew, Yiddish and Russian inscriptions.

These sights worked wonders on my memory. As I
remembered more details, I talked more. Jeff's camcorder
was running. My children's curiosity and profound interest in

every detail was comforting and gratifying. Their knowledge and understanding made them into true inheritors of this cruel legacy. This will not be a distant intellectual knowledge but one they appreciate in its full emotional dimension.

Miriam expressed this when she was fourteen years old with a poem she wrote after she came home from religion school:

> I am so angry
> I felt like screaming,
> You are taking part of
> Me, of my life
> And trying to put it into words
> And theories.
> When my father went
> Back to his hometown
> The temple was gone,
> A warehouse was in its place,
> My father never cries
> But when he saw his temple
> Destroyed
> A part of him died ...
>
> Now and then an image
> Comes to my mind
> Of a temple
> Burned out, missing a wall
> The broken shape of a
> Jewish star
> mutilated.

We were now standing in front of the steps leading to one of the gas chambers. On the top of these steps rest the ruins of the crematoria the Germans had blown up as the Russian army was approaching in January 1945. Since then, nobody seems to have touched these chunks of cement and twisted iron. One cannot make out the structure of any of the crematoria nor their relationship to the gas chambers, but the steps leading to the underground where people had to undress are clearly visible. As I was standing there, Sharone wanted to take a picture of me because, she said, "These are the steps my mother did not walk down on."

Passing on our history in this setting did not only bring me relief. We all felt strangely content. We realized just how comforting this experience was when, after returning to Krakow, we played with Zach and Noah at the dinner table. We all were in a remarkably good mood. Being with our grandchildren, anticipating the births of two more, filled us with great appreciation for life; our gratitude for having a new and beautiful family had deepened with this trip. Sharone's statement had attained an additional meaning.

We returned to Auschwitz two years later with Rafael and Susannah and their two-year-old son, Nicholas. This time Susanna was pregnant with our fifth grandchild, Jeremy. Again, it was the presence of our children and the chance to share our memories with them that provided a soothing background for the profound grief such visits awaken.

staircase

———

A PILGRIMAGE

We left Munich and headed toward Mauthausen, a concentration camp in Upper Austria, about two hundred kilometers from Vienna. Driving from Germany, we approached the camp from the west. The Hungarian Jewish men, on a death march in the fall and winter of 1944, came from the east, and so we were not traveling the same route. Still, as we drove through the well-tended fields and neat little villages, we tried to imagine how thousands of men with little food and water reached their destination. Among the men were our uncles and cousins, friends, Paul's forty-eight-year-old father, and my twenty-year-old brother, Andrew.

As we drove, we asked ourselves many questions that had never occurred to us before. How long did it take them to get to Mauthausen from the various forced labor camps scattered throughout Hungary, Czechoslovakia, and Poland? Did it take weeks? Did it take months? How could they survive the bitter cold without adequate shoes and clothing? What happened to those who died on the way? Where did they sleep? What did they eat? Did they march on the highways, or were they driven through forests and fields? Did the people living in these well-kept houses in this magnificent pastoral setting see this discarded mass of people? And if they did, what did they make of it? Did they care?

The stone quarry in Mauthausen was established as a concentration camp shortly after the Germans annexed Austria in September 1938. Mauthausen became one of the most feared camps in occupied Europe. Even the inmates of Auschwitz dreaded the possibility of being sent there.

There were over 200,000 people imprisoned in Mauthausen and its forty-nine sub-camps. At the time of liberation in May 1945 approximately 81,000 emaciated men and women were found here, most of them sick and dying. Because of the total absence of hygiene, terrible overcrowding, and many years of starvation, most of the prisoners had died, as did my brother, in a fast-spreading typhus epidemic.

At first the camp mainly held criminals and prisoners of war, who constructed the stone housing for the SS guards and the wooden barracks for Jews and political prisoners. Toward the end of the war, however, when many camps were threatened by the advancing Allied armies, camps like Auschwitz, Bergen-Belsen, Ravensbrueck and Gross-Rosen emptied their human cargo into Mauthausen.

Passing through the picturesque small town of Mauthausen with its Gothic church built in 1400, we arrived at the campsite and were surprised to find several large tourist busses parked there. They carried mainly school children from Germany and Austria, but we also saw tourists from Poland, Italy, and other parts of Europe. Not only Jews were intermed in this Camp. There were political prisoners from approximately twenty European countries shared the camp with the Jews.

We first walked into a rectangular courtyard that was surrounded by what looked like stables or garages. Indeed, this was where the SS guards kept their cars in working order. The number of guards grew from a little over one thousand in 1938 to close to ten thousand by the end of the war.

From here, we walked up some stairs and saw a huge statue. The face and part of the shoulders of a stern-looking man had been carved out, while the rest of the body remained encased in the roughly hued white stone. The statue commemorates a Russian general who was put to death by being made to stand in below-freezing weather while cold water was poured over him. Freezing the man to death appeared to have been a revenge for the death of the many German soldiers who froze to death in Russia during the winter of 1943. If this is what they did to a prisoner of war, how did they torture the Jews, the most despised of all of the Nazi's "enemies"?

We entered the campground proper and tried to put ourselves back in time, which we did without difficulty. We filled the clean-scrubbed barracks and the outdoors with masses of emaciated, unshaven men in striped prison pajamas. We looked into their hollow eyes and saw resignation and terror. We saw them standing for roll call or shuffling about in their ill-fitting shoes. Those too weak to stand crouched on the ground in semi-consciousness.

We wanted to see everything and learn as much as possible about this place. We visited every barrack, every site of horror. As we looked at the double-stacked bunk beds and the outdoor areas which, by the time the Hungarian Jewish men were brought here, must have been filled with the sick and the dying, I tried to picture the spot where my genteel brother Andrew may have died. His image lingered with me the entire time we traveled here, but I felt it most strongly when we were inside the camp. Later, when we discovered a few tombstones erected on the place where the barracks for the sick used to be, I realized that my quest to know how and where he died was not unusual. Others, too, had come here with such thoughts in their minds.

In "The Backpack," I described the last time I saw my brother and how my mother and I packed his backpack with great care, not knowing where he was going or how long his ordeal would last. When Andrew was caught trying to escape with a cousin and the two young men were handed over to the Hungarian police, they were taken to Mauthausen and almost certain death.

Mauthausen was not technically considered an extermination camp, but in its gas chamber and crematoria, at its punishment wall and in its granite stone quarry, people died here almost as efficiently as they did in extermination camps.

The extent of destruction in Mauthausen became clear to us when we left the barracks and walked into the sculpture garden, which contained monuments from Poland, Russia, Holland, Hungary, and Yugoslavia—the countries whose sons and daughters died in this place. In a prominent location, at the edge of the plateau, stands the monument for the Jewish victims: a huge, seven-pronged menorah with twisted branches. Next to it, written in Modern Hebrew letters, is the word "*zachor*," meaning "remember." This monument overlooks the rolling hills and well-kept farmhouses. From its position, one gets the feeling that it cries out to the world to remember what happened here, to remember that this beautiful and peaceful place at one time was the site of unimaginable suffering, torture, and horror.

Walking away from the sculpture garden, we spotted the infamous staircase of Mauthausen, the Staircase of Death. Before reaching the stairs, we looked down a granite cliff descending about one hundred feet to the bottom of the stone quarry. Under the granite wall, the pit was filled with ground water. This place was called the Parachute Leap because inmates were either thrown down to their death, or the lucky ones jumped themselves and were able to "parachute" to death.

We were now standing at the top of the infamous steps and looked down on a wide staircase which, toward the bottom, became even wider and reached the floor of the quarry with an almost elegant slight curve. The stairs are no longer in their original form; they are no longer as high and no longer in the same disarray as when the prisoners were made to go up and down on them; they are now easier to climb.

People called this area the Staircase of Death because prisoners were made to march down the steps into the quarry, where guards strapped a stone weighing about fifty kilograms onto their backs. The prisoners were then made to then march up the stairs in rows of five. The weak ones, who could not walk with stones that were, in many cases, heavier than their body weight, were beaten. Totally exhausted, unable to climb the stairs, they would fall backward and the whole column behind them would plummet to their deaths.

As I went down these stairs a young couple walked around quietly holding hands. Few people come down here; the 186 stairs are not easy to climb even without a stone strapped to your back. How did it feel to march them on a hot day or on a very cold one? We left Mauthausen with our hearts heavier than when we arrived. The stones were not on our shoulders; they were lodged in our hearts. We knew of the Nazis intention to exterminate the Jews and their other internal enemies, but we did not know the extent of the brutality that they exercised on their victims. We did not know about the amount of torture our people had to suffer before they were finally allowed to die.

WEIMAR AND BUCHENWALD:
TWO FACES OF GERMANY

On the Appellplatz[1] where, on April 19, 1945, the survivors of
Buchenwald assembled to pay final tribute to their dead comrades,
there is a rough, unpolished stainless steel plaque with the names
of the fifty-one countries whose sons and daughters were brought
here to work and to die. Other than Jews, there were partisans,
resistance fighters and prisoners of war imprisoned and killed
here in great numbers. There were also nine hundred children
in the camp saved mainly by members of the French resistance
movement.

154   We reached Buchenwald from Weimar, one of Germany's
most attractive small towns in Thuringen. According to the
archives, Germans had lived in Weimar since the early part of the
fourteenth century. Buchenwald has a much shorter history. It was
built in 1937 on the northern hill of Ettersberg where, in better
days, among the beautiful trees, the citizens of Weimar had their
picnics, drank their beer and ate their salami sandwiches.

Buchenwald, one of the first concentration camps built in
Germany, is only eight kilometers from Weimar. In the second half
of the 1930s, concentration camps sprang up all over the country,
their numbers rapidly increasing after the beginning of the war.
With the swift occupation of so many countries in 1941 and 1942,
there was not enough space to house the Jews, the communists,
the Gypsies, the criminals, the homosexuals and all those who
were "undesirable encumbrances" to Germany's National Socialist
regime. In Poland and the Ukraine, sonderkommandos sprayed

their victims with automatic weapons into mass graves, but this practice could not do the job with sufficient speed and efficiency, and so a cleaner and speedier way had to be found.

For this purpose, sixteen high-ranking SS officers met in January 1942 in an elegant villa along the shores of Wannsee. The meeting took ninety minutes. This is all the time they needed to approve the gas chambers, determine their locations and the means by which Jews would be collected and transported to the sites of extermination. The visit to the Wannsee House, which is now a museum, helped us understand the bureaucratic machinery involving every strata of Germany's municipal and state administration. We could see how these hierarchically organized bureaucracies secured obedience and created the zeal with which the perpetrators performed their macabre tasks throughout the war. Some of the SS officers who made these fateful decisions were re-appointed to various positions in the post-war German government; very few were punished for their crimes.

But I don't want to tell you about all the places that we feel compelled to visit whenever we are in Europe. This story is about Weimar and Buchenwald. Because of their physical proximity, they best symbolize Germany's Janus face.

As we approached Weimar by car, we could see from the highway a massive tower: the Monument of Buchenwald. Seeing the monument high in the mountain overlooking the city, I thought that this monument always will be part of this landscape. The shadow of Buchenwald will fall forever on Weimar, on this city of poetry and music. From here on, nobody can think of Germany only as the country that gave the rest of Europe some of its most beautiful and most enduring music and literature. Nobody who sees this monument is allowed to forget that a short distance from the city with an extraordinarily rich cultural heritage stood a concentration camp where, over an eight-year period, nearly a hundred thousand people suffered the cruelest treatment in the history of Western Civilization. Toward the end of the war, when many camps were "threatened" by advancing Russian and American troops, Buchenwald became the end-station for many Jews who were on death marches from Auschwitz, Ravensbrueck, Gross-Rosen and other camps. In the winter of 1945 when these prisoners arrived here, thirteen thousand people died in a period of about one hundred days. The total number of people who died in Buchenwald will never be known but it is estimated to be about fifty-one thousand. At the time of liberation on April 11, 1945, the camp was ridden with dysentery and typhus; most of the twenty-one thousand people still alive were sick and reduced to skin and bones.

156

Though numbers never tell the full story, we spotted, among the many documents, an official report that gave us insight into the mentality of the perpetrators. The report was titled "Profit Calculation Regarding the Exploitation of the Prisoners." The calculation was based on an estimate that the average prisoner would live for nine months. Renting a prisoner to industry for six reichsmark for a day, out of which money for food (sixty pfennings) and clothing (ten pfennings, because the clothing was "amortized") was deducted, the net profit per prisoner for the nine-month period was estimated to be 1,431.00 reichsmark. Added to this profit were "the proceeds from efficient utilization of the dead bodies." Gold teeth, clothing, money, and other valuables taken from the prisoners upon arrival in camp were listed under this heading. The total profit for a nine-month period from all the camps came to fifty million German marks. The only deduction from this sum was the cost of burning the bodies, which was two reichsmark per body. Not included in this profit calculation "were proceeds from bones and utilization of ashes."

Walking these grounds and reading the many well-displayed documents in the museum, we could see the dirty and crowded accommodations; we could imagine what it was like to work fourteen to sixteen hours every day in a stone quarry, on building a road, or in an armament factory. And how can we forget the terrible hunger and the biting cold on the slopes of a hill in Northern Europe?

While still trying to comprehend the extent of hunger, physical suffering and torture that preceded the deaths of these people, we returned to Weimar, the town that is considered to be the birthplace of German culture, which influenced and determined the modern cultural life of Western Europe. This is the town where J.S. Bach played the organ in the local church and where one can visit the homes in which Goethe and Schiller lived. The city was also the home of Franz Liszt and Richard Strauss and where, at the end of "the golden epoch," the Bauhaus architect Gropius introduced modernism. The small town square includes the Bauhaus Museum and the National Theater, in front of which stands the famous twin statue of Goethe and Schiller. In 1999, Weimar was proclaimed the "culture capital" of Europe. Large-scale musical and theatrical performances were planned as well as exhibitions and workshops in every branch of the arts. From the tastefully prepared catalogue for these events I was particularly struck by the offering of a musical workshop with the title "Music between Culture and Anti-Culture." The participants in this workshop were young people from Israel, the Arab countries, from the Weimar Music Gymnasium and from the Franz Liszt Music

High School. The ten-day workshop was organized and led by Daniel Barenboim. The organizers of the festivities were trying to bridge the gulf between Weimar and Buchenwald; exhibitions from Weimar would travel to the museum in Buchenwald and artifacts from the camp would be exhibited in Weimar.

To me, the moral schism between these two worlds appeared unbridgeable, though there is evidence everywhere that Jews and young Germans are trying to reconcile the ghost of Buchenwald with the spirit of Weimar. We encountered this attitude throughout much of Germany. The grandchildren of the perpetrators are now in their twenties and thirties, and they feel free to ask questions. In order to liberate themselves from their parents' and grandparents' shameful past, they want to be informed. The effort to establish meaningful communication between Germans and Jews is most evident in Berlin. The American Jewish Congress opened an office here and the Jewish Community Center has a small but well-staffed and busy library that is also visited by students of a nearby university.

But the story of the recent past followed us everywhere. In the library of the Jewish Community Center in Berlin we saw a map of occupied Europe designed especially to illustrate the vastness of the Holocaust machinery: watchtowers indicating the presence of extermination camps, black circles of varying sizes (according to the size of the camp) designating the locations of camps and ghettos, small stars of David showing the sites where synagogues were burnt during Kristallnacht. The map was literally "blackened" with concentration camps and places where hatred and prejudice found their free expression. The map made me realize just how thoroughly the death factories were geographically integrated into the German landscape. Are there still Germans who maintain that they had no idea what was going on in their country during WW II?

This latest of our trips to Germany left me with the clear impression that while the festivities in Weimar may have made an effort to overcome the gulf between the legacy of Weimar and the legacy of Buchenwald, the reconciliation between Germans and Jews may only be possible with an ongoing dialogue and only between future generations.

The place for roll call.

DEDICATION

"To survivors, the permanent cording off of memory would
mean an ultimately tragic alienation from their history,
an excision of part of their identity, even if that is an
ineradicably hurtful part."
Eva Hoffman in her review of A. Appelfeld's *Beyond Despair,*
The New York Times, January 23, 1994

The chairs were wet, the mud was deep, the rain, with small
interruptions, was steady. People were not prepared for this
kind of weather at the end of April. Still, I heard only a few
complaints about the arrangement committee's failure to put up
tents on the lawn where the people attending the dedication of
the newly erected Holocaust Memorial Museum were sitting.
Most people huddled together and talked quietly in small
groups before the ceremony began. We had time to admire
the architecture of the museum that was highly praised in all
reviews. I had an especially strong visceral reaction to what
appeared to be watchtowers at the corners of this relatively
massive structure.

Once the ceremony began, our view was partially blocked
by umbrellas, and I heard comments about how one could see
more and would certainly be more comfortable had one stayed
home and watched the proceedings on television. But we were
glad we came; we were glad to be here in the company of other
survivors.

I looked around: this was definitely an aging group of

people. Many came with their families, with children and grandchildren. The mood was solemn but not depressed. If anything, it was somewhat upbeat. We came to witness an event that none of us thought possible fifty years ago. But here we were: in front of us a magnificent museum, next to it a simple but spacious building for the archives to document the events in Europe between 1933 and 1945.

After two hours of trying to keep ourselves relatively comfortable in the driving rain (the weather helped to make our memories more real), the ceremony began. Onto the platform came about ten heads of state with their wives, including Chaim Herzog of Israel, the vice president and president of the United States, and the survivors who were responsible for the creation of the museum. It was at that moment that I had an unexpected thought: this is our museum and we are giving it to the American people. There will be thousands and thousands of people who will come here to learn about the fate of the Jews of Europe; more people will know about our history than we had ever expected. I heard it many times repeated: "Tell it to the world, please tell everyone what happened to us." This was the most fervent wish of those who died. There are other Holocaust museums and monuments in this country but this museum is in a very special place, practically next door to the Washington Monument.

I had read a great deal about the Holocaust, heard many speeches and given quite a few myself. Still, I found the introduction by Ted Koppel, the address by Elie Wiesel, and the speech by President Clinton deeply moving. I was drawn to Ted Koppel in particular. I did not know he was a child of survivors. He made me think of my children, of the children of

all our survivor friends and all the Jewish children who could
have been. There are so many outstanding people among this
"second generation"; whenever I meet one of them, read their
books, hear their speeches it is then that I realize, once more,
the treasures we have lost.

The next day, we went into the museum. What the
reviews had failed to emphasize is the way that the interior
of the building is in perfect harmony with its exterior. Here,
too, every detail brought memories. Particularly impressive
was the elevator: as the heavy doors shut tight behind us, and
images appeared on a small video screen, I felt the terror of
"no-escape" in a way that surprised and frightened me. And
the attention to details! The glass walls of the corridors
connecting various parts of the building have the names
of every destroyed community engraved on them. Would
Szendro, the tiny Jewish community where I was born, be
listed here? Paul looked for Hajdunanas immediately. Why did
finding the names of these small Hungarian towns give us so
much satisfaction? The answer is simple: the Holocaust was
not only the destruction of individuals and whole families but
also thousands of Jewish communities. It is here that these
communities are memorialized.

As we left the museum, I felt immense gratitude; I was
grateful that the museum came into being while we were still
around to see it. I was particularly happy to know that it will
be here for my children to see, and that one day they will bring
their children here, the day when they will be old enough to
understand its meaning. This museum, as all other memorials,
will help our grandchildren know about the fate of their great
grandparents. Will they want to know it? And if they do, will

their lives be richer, their own sense of identity stronger, if they know of this terrible chapter in Jewish history? I hope so. As I delight in the kind of people our children have become and celebrate the birth of each new grandchild, my own memories of the past are becoming stronger, not dimmer. Erikson was right: "Within the life cycle, generativity is concerned with new beings as well as new products and new ideas and which, as a link between generations, is as indispensable for the renewal of the adult generation's own life as it is for that of the next generation."

Renewal is not forgetting; renewal comes from an ever-deeper appreciation of memories that link the past with the present. Our lives are finite but museums, monuments, books, letters, pictures, and stories told by parents to their children go on living—at least for a while. As grandparents, we had become increasingly more conscious of representing a very small link in the chain of generations of Jews that by miracle survived the attempt at all-out destruction. I am also extremely proud that our children had become heirs to the ethical and moral values that had guided many previous generations through their turbulent lives. Nothing could give us greater strength to face the infirmities and illnesses that are inevitable with age than this pride and this knowledge.

A REUNION

A remarkable reunion took place in Great Barrington, in
the beautiful Berkshires. We gathered on the lawn of the
summer home of dear friends, the Tuchmans, who provided
leadership to our group of men and women when we were
students in Heidelberg, between the years of 1945-1952.
The setting for our reunion was perfect. The Tuchmans had
created a magnificent memorial in the meadow of the property
surrounding their weekend home. Small steps lead down to a
graveled area, where six large boulders in their natural colors
and shapes had been placed with only one word in front of
them: "Zachor." On the side of the area, surrounded by trees
and small bushes, are the dates 1939-1945, along with a small
Magen David made out of steel nails. Every piece is filled
with symbolism, and every word has meaning that needed no
explanation for the members of this group.

Most of the twenty or so people who gathered on that
Fourth of July weekend in 1995 were teenagers in Poland when
the war broke out. Some were born and raised in Hungary,
and two women were young children in Germany when Hitler
came to power. Most married other survivors, while a few had
American spouses.

The conversations were filled with fervent emotions.
We not only wanted to find out about everyone's children
and grandchildren, we also asked questions we did not ask
of each other in Heidelberg. How come we knew so little
about the way each of us survived? There may have been

an assumption—not a correct one—that we all suffered a similar fate. Our fates were similar only as far as the loss of our families, our communities, and our homes were concerned. Even within Poland, people suffered in different ways. Some escaped into Russia and were imprisoned in camps there. Others, who could not escape, survived in hiding. Still others lived through many years in various concentration camps or fought in the underground. The fate of the Hungarian Jews differed from that of the Polish Jews, because large scale deportations did not begin in Hungary until 1944.

Where did these people go after liberation? What were their physical conditions? I learned that some had gone to Heidelberg directly from concentration camps, mainly from Bergen-Belsen, which became a refugee camp after its liberation by the British. Others had gone to look for family and relatives. Some had tried to go to Palestine but, because of the English blockade, returned to West Germany.

What I learned about their lives since our student days made me very proud to be a member of this little club, the first Jewish Student Union of Heidelberg after twelve years of Nazi rule. At least three members of this small group made it to the pinnacle of their professions: an economist, a mathematician and a biochemist. The rest of us were either in full-time or part-time academic positions, spent our lives in the private practice of medicine, or built new lives in various forms of business.

But the greatest pride we felt was not in our own accomplishments but in the personal qualities of our children. Only a few children of the next generation attended. Their presence made a big difference to all of us. They were thoughtful, affectionate young men and women, many of them professionally accomplished in their own right. Where were the emotional scars that we were supposed to have inflicted on them? Rather than depression and nihilism, even casual observation indicated that most of these young people lived with a remarkable degree of vitality. It appeared that our experiences did not rob them of their ability to prepare themselves for useful and creative lives.

In camps and in ghettos, people lived under conditions not meant for human existence. We were stripped of the trimmings of civilized life. Upon our return to civilization, we rediscovered the simple joys of everyday life; the joy of waking up in our own beds, the joy of a hot shower, the joy of eating nourishing, tasty meals. The joy of knowing that when we become sick, we will be cared for, and when the time comes, we will die a human death and will be buried in our individual graves. My children and my friends' children tell me that this particular feature of their survivor-parents impressed them most. They learned from their parents that the everyday joys of life should not be taken for granted. I believe that our struggles for survival may have taught our children to value life more fully and that in all of life what counts is the sharing of life. Many were deeply committed to improving the lives of others. "Tikkun Olam," the idea that all of us ought to feel obliged to repair an imperfect world, had attained great meaning for many young Jews after the Holocaust. A large number of them had gone into the helping professions.

And how do we understand and explain our readiness to turn our attention to our studies so soon after the war? What accounts for this stubborn capacity of Jews to move forward while looking back, as they appear preoccupied with their past? Many people had looked at this question and among the many explanations there was one suggesting that there may be something peculiar to the Jewish mind. Do Jews really have a peculiar brain? Do they posses peculiar mental resources? At times it appeared so, especially between the years of 1860-1930, a period of seventy years.

This was the period when emancipation in most European countries permitted the Jews to leave the confines of their ghettos and enter universities, the professions, and various businesses. Once Emancipation opened the doors of universities (never completely, because there always was some sort of numerus clausus, except in Italy), the sons of Talmud scholars were ready for the challenge. When considering the level and kind of contributions that Jews had made in German-speaking Europe during the relatively brief period of time between 1860 and 1930 to the sciences, literature, and the performing arts, it would be easy to reach the conclusion that there is indeed something special to the Jewish brain. It is good for Jewish pride, especially at times of severe persecution, to be reminded of the fact that before WW II, in Germany, where they comprised about three quarters of one percent of the population, Jews constituted twenty-five percent of the most distinguished mathematicians, physicists, and medical researchers. Also, according to Stefan Zweig, himself a famous Austrian-Jewish writer, nine-tenths of what would be celebrated as "Viennese culture" was promoted, nourished, and created by Viennese Jewry.

However, I believe, there is nothing biological about these facts. The answer likely is that if a large number of Jews

displayed great competence and often, great originality, it
was due to the historic circumstances that made survival of a
disproportionately large number of intelligent Jews possible.
Jews may not be possessors of a distinctly Jewish mind, but
they are a group of people whose life is the life of the mind,
if only because over the centuries they had, for the most part,
little direct contact with the earth.

Our desire and determination to go to a university,
to acquire intellectual skills and knowledge, I believe, was
deeply embedded in our Jewish heritage. Our studies had
roots emotionally and intellectually in a foundation that was
built over many generations and over many centuries. This
foundation had now become a springboard from which a group
of young Jewish men and women could embark on a new life.

Another question seemed relevant at the reunion: How
do we explain the strong bonds we built with each other in
the relatively short period of time we shared in Heidelberg?
Was this the same as when friendships develop in college and
become precious to people because of the intense emotions that
characterize college life? Perhaps.

But this was not ordinary college life. We were a group
of young Jews at a German university. We were surrounded
by a population that followed a leader who was determined to
exterminate us and did successfully annihilate almost all our
contemporaries and all our families. We lived in the homes of
SS men who were still in American prisoner-of-war camps, in
the homes of National Socialists and, rarely, in the homes of
Social Democrats. We had gotten to know Germans of various
political persuasions, including an extraordinary clergyman,
Kreisdekan Herman Maas, who was part of an anti-Nazi

underground and help rescue Jewish children into Palestine.

I am frequently asked why we had gone to Germany after our experiences during the war. Such questions make me realize how little was known about the condition of the Jewish survivors following the war years. It is not known generally that for the first three years after the war, until 1948, only fifty thousand Jews entered the United States because immigration visas were granted in keeping with the quotas of the survivors' countries of origin, and countries like Poland and Hungary had very low immigration quotas. The majority of survivors came to the United States after June 1948, when the first Displaced Persons Act was passed in Congress, allowing two hundred thousand Jews and non-Jewish refugees to enter. This number still was extremely low, given the actual need, and eventually was expanded in 1950 to 415,744.

After liberation, we either could stay in Eastern Europe, which was occupied by the Soviet Union and governed by restrictive, anti-Semetic Communist regimes, or find our way to the Western part of Europe that was occupied by the Allied Military Forces. After we crossed the border illegally between East and West (many of us with the help of the Jewish underground), we headed toward the refugee camps, most of which were set up in Bavaria and supported by the United Nations Relief Agency (UNRA) and the Joint Distribution Committee. In the camps we learned that speedy immigration was not possible, and so we had made every effort to be admitted to a university. We knew that with some exception, the professors who taught us were members of the Nazi party. We knew our classmates had been soldiers on one of the many fronts or could have actively participated in the destruction of our families. I believe we made a wise decision to immigrate to the United States with our various diplomas, because none of us could have afforded an education at an American university.

In Germany, our Jewish Student Union constituted an island that provided security, love, and friendship. At the reunion, I was extremely pleased when many spoke with a great deal of affection of my mother who cooked the noon meals for us. We looked forward to this one hot meal of the day in the little house next to the Jewish Community Center. Here, in each other's company, we resumed practicing, in some rudimentary form, the traditions in which we grew up and we began to celebrate our holidays. The feelings we developed toward each other were attempts to bring back the feeling of warmth and a sense of belonging that we craved after the loss of our families. The Yiddish and Hebrew songs we sang and taught each other created an ambiance in which deep attachments could flourish. And now, our children having become professionals themselves and many of us having become grandparents, we came back to bask in the warmth which, after the big catastrophe, helped us regain our emotional strength.

Acknowledgments

My deepest gratitude goes to my first audience, the people who sat around our Seder table over a forty-year period. These were our children— Sharone, Miriam and Rafael—and our closest and dearest friends, Steve and Lusia Hornstein and their three children, Mark, Frank and Ruth. Originally, the stories were not intended for publication; they were in the oral history tradition.

With time, the children were joined by their spouses and their children. Their responses and those of many of our friends encouraged me to add a new story year after year. Everyone around the table listened with rapt attention: the eagerness with which they wanted to learn about our tragic history on the occasion of the celebration of the Exodus from Egypt forged an extraordinary intergenerational bond. I hope that the publication of the book will make it possible for others to have similar experiences; to learn about the every-day struggles for survival that had to be fought in all extermination and concentrations camps. The struggles for survival were most valiantly fought by my mother; she is the hero in many of the stories.

I want to thank Mr. Richard Hunt, President of Emmis Books, for recognizing the value of these personal stories for a larger audience and to thank Mr. Jack Heffron for his editorial help. I am very grateful to my collaborator, Mr. Stewart Goldman, for the etchings that accompany the stories. Stewart's appreciation of the personal nature of the stories helped me overcome my initial doubts about their meaning to a larger audience.

Anna Ornstein

My Mother's Eyes is a memoir of the experiences of Dr. Anna Ornstein, a Holocaust survivor. I became drawn to the Holocaust through my own personal experience. Last night, while discussing this interest with my wife, Kristi, she commented on my feelings of persecution in the late seventies that precipitated the making of *The Last of the Sabine Women* and then immediately after, the paintings *Chambers I through VII*, which were completed in 1981-82 and reflected on the Holocaust.

In 1985, I exhibited the Chamber paintings in conjunction with a YomHaShoah service. Anna saw the paintings for the first time and was drawn to them immediately because they seemed to connect directly with her experience in the concentration camps. She commented on the sound of boots that she seemed to hear and on the raw architecture in the spaces depicted in the paintings. We established a dialogue that brought us together roughly eleven years later, when she approached me with her stories and asked about my interest in illustrating them. I met with Mark Patsfall of Mark Patsfall Press, to enlist his support in renewing my limited knowledge of the etching process. The images reproduced in *My Mother's Eyes* reflect the expertise and care that he and Mark Cowgill brought to the printing of my etchings for the portfolio *Tales of Slavery and Deliverance*, published in 1997. To this day, I remain greatly appreciative of the dedication and sensitivity they both brought to the making of that portfolio.

There have been numerous other people who have aided my efforts in the making of images related to the Holocaust for whom I am greatly thankful. Toni Laboiteax who has supported my work for many years was the first to exhibit the Chamber paintings in her gallery in Cincinnati in 1982. B.J. Foreman, Owen Findsen and Maureen Bloomfield wrote about the Chamber paintings and other works in various formats and have always been supportive of my efforts. Likewise, I remain indebted to Randy Sandler, Cincinnati Art Galleries, who exhibited the Chamber paintings and the Cherubs installation; to Michael Solway who first exhibited the portfolio in his gallery in 1997, committing to it before it was even finished; and to Peter Pinnau of the Kulturreferat in Munich, Germany, who was instrumental in arranging exhibitions for the Portfolio in Munich and Wiesbaden, Germany. I thank Dick Rosenthal for his interest in the portfolio and for presenting it to Richard Hunt; this gesture enabled the eventual publishing of the book.

And finally the staunchest and most honest critics and supporters of my work have been my wife Kristi, my daughter Annika, and my son Daniel, whose eyes and feelings have often enabled a clearing of my vision.

Stewart Goldman

DR. ANNA ORNSTEIN is an Auschwitz survivor, professor of child psychology at Harvard University and is professor emeritus of child psychiatry at the University of Cincinnati. She lives in Brookline, Massachusetts.

STEWART GOLDMAN is an award-winning artist and teacher of international renown. His work has been exhibited throughout the United States, the Ukraine and Germany for over four decades. He retired from the Art Academy of Cincinnati in 2001, where he was a professor of painting. Born and educated in Philadelphia, Stewart has lived in Cincinnati since 1968.